Reg Thompson

Reg Thompson lives with his wife, Hilary, and their two sons, Robbie and Harry, in Newport, Essex.

Dear Charlie

Letters to a Lost Daughter

REG THOMPSON

JOHN MURRAY

First published in Great Britain in 2006 by John Murray (Publishers)
A division of Hodder Headline

Paperback edition 2007

A CIP catalogue record for this title is available from the British Library

ISBN 978-0-7195-6350-8

Typeset in Bembo by Hewer Text UK Ltd, Edinburgh
Printed and bound by Clays Ltd, St Ives plc

Hodder Headline's policy is to use papers that are natural,
renewable and recyclable products and made from wood grown
in sustainable forests. The logging and manufacturing processes are expected
to conform to the environmental regulations of the country of origin.

John Murray (Publishers)
338 Euston Road
London NW1 3BH

*For Charlie who dances on the wind
and for my wife Hilary and my two beautiful sons,
Robbie and Harry, who are equally loved.*

Preface

At around 6.30 in the morning on 3 December 2005 I walked quietly into my daughter's bedroom. She was asleep, curled up on her side, her face towards the wall. Her bear, Bongos, lay firm within her grasp and her duvet, for the most part, was on the floor. I leant forward to kiss her on the forehead and as I did so she rolled over on to her back. As my face came towards hers, her eyes opened, a brief moment of incomprehension was replaced by a slow smile.

'Bye-bye, sweetheart,' I said. 'Be careful in Cambridge. Take care crossing the road and don't speak to strangers.'

'I love you, Daddy,' she said and with that she rolled over again and disappeared back into her dreams.

I picked the duvet up from the floor and carefully placed it over her. On my way out of the house I looked in on my two sons, Robbie and Harry (or Horsey), both soundly asleep and beyond disturbance. I could throw a bucket of water over Harry in his sleep and it would not wake him.

Charlie had made me promise the night before that I would say goodbye to her before I went to work. After all, she was used to getting up early. Every Saturday for the previous six months she had accompanied me to work, a wonderful companion and diligent co-worker, at thirteen as enthusiastic and committed as any of the other employees in my brother Davy's wholesale delicatessen business. Some had rechristened her Charlie Muscles, in awe of her ability to carry two five-kilo tubs of olives in either hand.

On Saturday, 3 December 2005 Charlie had finally earned enough money to do her Christmas shopping. She planned to leave on the 10.42 train from Elsenham station with her friend Livvy and travel to Cambridge. Although neither my wife, Hilary, nor I knew Livvy, we were aware that she used the train every day to travel to school. Of all the dangers that our vivid and overwrought imaginations could predict, the perils of the station lay disguised and overlooked. The great majority of Charlie's friends used the train regularly, either for school or to meet their friends at weekends.

By 8.30 a.m. I had loaded my van and was preparing to set out. I remember it being a fine day, of beautiful sunshine interrupted by intermittent cloud. At around 11.30 I tried to ring Charlie to check that she had arrived safely in Cambridge and to tell her that I missed her. She didn't answer.

In attempting to catch the 10.42 Cambridge-bound train, Charlie and her friend Livvy had been struck by the southbound Stansted Express. According to the police, both girls died instantly. It was not their fault. They had not been 'messing about'. They had not attempted to run in front of an oncoming train. They bought their tickets from the ticket office on the London-bound platform and then crossed through the unlocked wicket gates with the idea of catching the train standing at the northbound platform. The miniature warning lights were still flashing, which we now understand to mean the imminent arrival of a second train. The reports into the accident suggest that the girls thought that the lights referred to the train already in the station. There was no 'fast train approaching' sign and no guard to warn them. Moreover, the oncoming train was hidden from view by the train standing at the platform. The Stansted Express hurtled through the station at a speed in excess of seventy miles an hour. The driver had recently been told not to sound his horn because of complaints from local residents. Charlie and Livvy had no chance.

I find it very difficult to write about what happened that day. Eight months on, we are still trapped in the surreal nightmare that descended upon us on that fateful morning. For the first month after the accident we were never alone. Friends, relatives, kindly strangers, all manner of people, beat a constant path to our door. The madness was kept at bay by a miraculous outpouring of love.

In early January, quite naturally, many people had to resume their normal lives. What had been a torrent of people reduced to a trickle. Our great friends, even now, barely dare to leave us alone for more than a couple of days, but still, we found ourselves, for much of the time, suffocated by disbelief and desperation. Hilary disappeared into a well of misery, barely able to speak or function but still able to show the courage needed to support our two wonderful sons. For me, then, as it is now, and as I know it will always be, I must find a way to keep a connection with my daughter. I began to write to her, talking to her as if she was away on holiday or at boarding school, keeping her up to date with the small events of an ordinary life. Above all I wanted to tell her how much I love her, how much I will always love her. It became and remains an obsession. When I write I am with her, surrounded by her presence, immersed in memories of her.

The letters were never written for publication. By the middle of April I had completed more than 50,000 words. My mother, whom I refer to in the letters as 'Oma', was aware of my writing and, gently but persuasively, she prevailed upon me to read what I had written. At first I shied away from the idea. The letters were and are personal, compiled without thought for any other reader and not always complimentary. Oma was deeply moved and distressed. Even she had been unable to comprehend the depths of our misery. Very soon afterwards, I gave the incomplete letters to another friend, known affectionately to us as Mel C. She read nearly 200 pages in one three-hour sitting and then rang me straightaway. 'Publish them,' she said. 'They will help others.'

I do not know what is right and what is wrong. I know that suffering is universal and that it is more common to be touched by tragedy than to escape it.

Reg Thompson
Newport, Essex
31 July 2006

Family and Friends

We moved to the area where we now live in the summer of 1995, although in the intervening time we have lived in several different houses, almost as if we have been checking out each village to find the one that suited us best. Robbie (now sixteen) immediately began his schooling at the Henham and Ugley Church of England Primary School. A year later Charlie joined her brother, leaving only Harry (Horsey) at home until the autumn of 1998. (He is now almost twelve.)

We met most of our closest friends through our children, afternoons spent waiting in the school playground, idle chat by the school gates. From such small beginnings wonderful friendships can be made.

I have put our friends together under headings to help identify them and to make clear their relationship both to us and to Charlie.

Henham School

The Wiggetts

Jill and Alan, and their children, Harry and Tom. Tom is the same age as Robbie and although they rarely see each other now, they were friends at primary school. Harry Wiggett was in Charlie's class at Henham. Charlie loved Jill's sense of humour and they shared a real lust for life.

The Bowes

Paul and Mel, and their children, Beck and Miles. Beck is four years older than Charlie but as families we became close quickly. Charlie looked up to Beck and Beck assumed the role of older sister. They were immensely fond of each other. Miles and Robbie were inseparable at primary school and, although they have drifted apart as their interests have steered them in different directions, they remain friends.

The Farrs

Suzanne, Dick and their son Jonny. Jonny and Horsey became friends at Henham school and have remained friends although they now go to different schools.

The Jameses

Terry and Sylvie, and their son, Frank. Frank and Horsey were great friends at school.

Hannah Pallet, Robyn Dane and Leanna Baldwin

Charlie's best friends at Henham School.

Mrs Dunn

Deputy headteacher at Henham School, and Charlie's favourite.

Debden Green

We lived in Debden Green, which is a tiny hamlet near Saffron Walden, before moving two miles down the road to Thaxted in December 2004.

The Nimmos

Mel and Andy, and their son, Harry. They are our neighbours, with whom we have become great friends. Charlie used to call in on Mel on her way home from school and insist on making cakes in her kitchen. We have always known Mel as Mel C so that we can tell the difference between the two Mels, the other one being Mel Bowe who is sometimes known as Mel B. This was an old Spice Girls joke that Charlie particularly enjoyed.

Jim Lamb

Jim was the first person we met when we moved to Debden Green in 1998. He lived next door to us in what used to be the old service station. I think Jim used to frighten Charlie a little when she was very young but he was tremendously fond of her.

Suzanne Darling

A friend and neighbour.

Our Relations

Oma

My mother. Oma is the familiar Dutch term for grandmother. Oma is Dutch, obviously, which makes me half Dutch and Charlie a quarter Dutch. Oma lives in Sudbury, a market town about twenty miles away. She adored Charlie and Charlie adored her.

Uncle Davy and Auntie Trish

My brother and my sister-in-law. They live near Colchester, about an hour's drive away. They lost their eldest son, Dan, in a car accident almost exactly a year before we lost Charlie. They have three other children, Simon, Jamie and Francesca. Charlie was very close to all her cousins. At Dan's funeral she read aloud a poem which she had written herself.

Auntie Franky

My sister who has lived in Rome for nearly thirty years. We see her once a year at best.

Auntie Jill, and her three sons, Toby, Oliver and Patrick

Jill is my wife's sister and the three boys are now in their twenties. They live near Manchester. Charlie loved them all.

Cousin Kate and her partner, Roger

Kate is Hilary's cousin. Roger lost his own son, Justin, eight months before we lost Charlie.

Uncle Ted

Hilary's uncle by marriage and cousin Kate's father.

Newport

When Robbie and, later, Charlie went up to Newport School to start their secondary education, our children made a whole new set of friends.

The McPartlands and their children, Charlie and Clare

Charlie is in the band with Robbie and we have become good friends with his parents Yvonne and Peter. Although the McPartlands met our daughter Charlie on several occasions, our friendship has grown since the accident.

Adele Meader, her children, Beth and Christopher, and her sister Rebecca (known to Charlie as Becka)

Beth, known as Bee, was a great friend of Charlie's at Newport school.

The Newport Kids (Robbie's Friends)

Cheese

Robbie's girlfriend. She won't let me tell you her real name. She immediately took to Charlie, and Charlie loved the fact that she could be such good friends with an older girl. The friendship between Charlie and Cheese brought Charlie and Robbie much closer together.

Chitson, Calvert, Gary, Fleetwood, Connor, Sam, Lou, Liv, Matt, James and Dean, Liam, Spuggy, Clayden, Will, the Newport Massif and any others I have forgotten to mention

Robbie's friends in year eleven. They all took to Charlie and made her feel special.

Work

My friends from when I had a proper job in the eighties, working for Warner Home Video designing video sleeves and posters.

John Keeling, David Rozalla and Murray Cameron

We all worked together from about 1984 onwards. Only Murray really knew Charlie. When she was very young she would play with Murray's daughter, Madeleine, as we lived quite close to each other. David met Charlie twice, I think. John never met Charlie.

Uncle Stu

His real name is Stuart Copland. He used to come and stay with us for so long that the children thought he must be a relation. Stu is also a work friend from my days at Warner.

Dr Mike Tayler

Our doctor in Thaxted. We owe Doctor Tayler a debt of gratitude for his compassion and kindness.

The Reverend Richard Titford

We asked Reverend Titford to take Charlie's service. We did not really know him but he took Dan's service and showed great kindness to Charlie when she stood in front of 700 people to read her poem. He has become a friend and comes regularly just to talk and to encourage us to believe in Charlie's spirit.

Robbie Gladwell

We met Robbie after Dan died. He is a musician with a studio near Sudbury. Charlie liked him straightaway and we were invited to his studio on several occasions. He played live at Charlie's service.

The Bazlintons

Tina and Chris, and their surviving daughter Stevie. Her sister, Livvy, was Charlie's friend. Chris has worked tirelessly to push through safety improvements at Elsenham station.

Hello, Charlie,

Not much has happened today. Mummy is washing the kitchen, throwing away some dead flowers and picking out live ones to make up new bunches. She hasn't said very much. I cuddle her as much as I can. Robbie went to London with Cheese and Sam and Calvert. They are going to Camden market. You would love it. Lots of stalls selling bohemian clothes and handmade jewellery, posters of dead pop stars and belts with bright, sparkly buckles.

Horsey slept until midday on the floor in the living room. That's where we've all been sleeping since you went away. I can't talk about you as if you aren't coming back. I can't say 'used' or 'loved' or any word ending in 'd'. You are alive to me although I know I won't be able to hug you again. I hug you all the time. I sit in the car holding your hand as I drive to the Spar or on my way to Newport to pick up Robbie. I see you, head up against the window, your thumb firmly in your mouth, answering my endless questions with an 'uh' or a 'shut it'. I listen and hear you say, 'Thaxted church spire,' with your thumb still clenched between your teeth. You never let me down. Not ever.

Jo Pallet offered to take Horsey to the cinema to see

Chronicles of Narnia. He's seen it twice already and didn't like it much either time. It was nice of Jo though. Auntie Trish calls it *Nadia.* I wonder if she does it on purpose. Horsey was horrified that there was a film about the man/woman who appeared on *Big Brother.* 'Why have they made a film about Nadia?' he said. 'I don't understand it.' There are a lot of things I don't understand.

Mummy just went upstairs. I won't leave her too long. She lies on your bed sometimes or stands in the middle of your room. Nothing has been touched. Robbie won't let any of his friends even go into your room. He is quiet in his grief but desperate. Sometimes he just takes my hand and squeezes it as hard as he can.

'You all right?' he says.

'Yes,' I say, although I will never be all right.

Horsey seems to have abandoned the few social skills he once had. He never talks about what happened and he seems, on the surface, to be fine but he has built around himself a wall like Helms Deep, keeping the darkness out. I watch him all the time just in case. He has seen too much for a boy of nearly twelve.

Christmas has passed. It is a small mercy. The house has been full of almost all the people we have ever known. One day we had Big Terry [James], Alan Wiggett and Heath all in the kitchen at the same time. Mummy and I had to stand outside. Auntie Trish and Auntie Jill cooked and cleaned, and brought glasses and plates and huge bags of food. Olly, Toby and Patrick stayed for more than a week, sleeping on the floor behind the sofa, playing chess with Horsey who beats everybody remorselessly. You would hate him for it although there is no doubt he is very good at it. I gave Bongos to Oma. Oma misses you so much.

Paul and Mel Bowe and Paul's father John have just arrived so I will stop now for a bit. We are going to walk up to Thaxted church and light a candle for you. Then we will probably go to the pub. I am going to ring Robbie and check he is all right. I know you know how much he loves you. I love you, darling.

Daddy

p.m.

Mel and Paul and John have just left. John is quite definitely mad. He told us a story about how he lost his luggage on a trip to Dublin two years ago. The only thing he could find was a pair of shoes. He sat in his hotel room for two days while the rest of his mates played pool and got drunk in the pub. Another time he managed to lose his underpants. I don't really know what happened as we all looked a bit embarrassed and John decided to tell another story about how he went to a wedding in a pair of trainers and his best suit. His life appears to be a catalogue of clothing disasters.

The house is quiet now. Mummy is on the phone to Auntie Jill and Horsey is playing Robbie's guitar. He can play 'When September Comes' by Green Day. Robbie is on his way back from London. I will have to go to Newport to pick him up soon. I can't bear the thought of not doing anything but most of the time I don't know what to do. We haven't got any food in the house except for a small packet of sausages and some soup. Mummy won't eat. We lit two candles for you.

Tomorrow I have to go to Sudbury to see Uncle Davy. I should be working even though Davy says I don't have to until I feel ready. It's not about that. I can't leave Mummy alone, and Robbie and Horsey go back to school on Wednesday. We'll think of something. It will be a month tomorrow. A lifetime. The days used to fly past, now they crawl like desperate old men. I used to think a lifetime was just that, seventy or eighty years. Now I know a lifetime can be a minute or a second or a month or thirteen years. I talk to you when I am in the car and in the mornings. I don't really say much, mostly that I love you. I love you so much.

Night-night.

Daddy

Hi, Charlikins,

I need to talk again. We have just watched *The Chronicles of Narnia* on a pirate DVD. Frankly I don't care. I don't even know if I should care. Anyway *The Chronicles of Narnia* was OK. *Lord of the Rings* it isn't but diverting enough. Mummy slept through it and Horsey kept calling the king a 'pussy', his new favourite word. I cried, not because of the film or only partly because of the film. Peter, the oldest boy, goes on and on about looking after the family, making sure that his brother and sisters are safe at any cost. I thought of you. I always think of you. I couldn't keep you safe. I can't go back. I can't change the past. I can't tumble out of a wardrobe and find myself a child again. I know what I have to do. I have to look after Mummy and Robbie and Horsey and probably Uncle Davy and Oma too. Uncle Davy says that your cousin Dan caught you as you fell. I don't believe him. You are my Charlie Muscles. You do the catching. Look after Dan for us too.

Robbie asked whether he could stay out late. I said yes so no surprise there. I'll have to drive to Newport at about 10.30. You will be with me as you were always with me. You even used to get out of bed and get dressed again to come with me. Nothing would stop you. I often had the nagging feeling that I wasn't quite being the sort of dad I should have been but I don't regret a moment. I only regret the moments I let you sleep or the times you decided you'd rather be with your friends. I've promised myself never to ask why or what if. I can't ask why. If I ask why I know I will go mad. There is no answer.

Do you remember Robbie Gladwell? He remembers you. He says that he can feel you. That you come to his studio and that his cats go crazy. He says you are happy. Mummy asked me whether I thought he was mad. He probably is mad. I want to be mad too. What's sane anyway? Believing in nothing. Saving for a pension. Paying off your credit cards. Doing well at school. Not littering. Calling people 'sir'. Buying a bigger house and wearing a suit. Sleeping in a bed. Sane people are mad.

Tubbs has crapped in the utility room again. The smell

is overpowering. I have to go and clear it up or we'll have to burn the house down. I also have to go to the shop to buy some burgers and oven chips. Horsey says he can't eat any more sausages. That gives you some idea as to just how many sausages he's eaten lately. Mummy says she will eat some soup.

I'm going now. I don't know if I'll write more tonight. If not, sleep well.

Bless you, my darling.

Daddy

Hello again, poppet,

I just needed to tell you something. I'm going to write down everything we ever did. Everything you ever did. I'm going to tell the world that I have the most beautiful, the most fantastic daughter who ever lived. I'm going to put your face in a million bookshops and on a million posters. You will live for ever. Robbie said you were too happy, that you had more happiness in thirteen years than most people have in a lifetime. I hope, I pray that it's true. Robbie Gladwell says that you have many secrets. Things were going on in your life that Mummy and I had no idea about. I hope he is right and I hope they were good things. I know that some of the girls in your year made you unhappy but you said you didn't care. I always thought you told me the truth. Please God let it be true that you really didn't care. Having to spend the whole summer with your father because not one girl in your year would speak to you. I don't know and I'll probably never know what happened but please let me know that it didn't make you unhappy. For me, this last summer was the best time of my whole life. I wouldn't change anything. I am so proud to be your father. So proud that you loved me and seemed to want to be with me.

I am sitting at my desk where you should be sitting, plugged into MSN talking to God knows who. I can see your face as I peer around the door, slightly guilty, grinning, quickly switching from whatever you were doing so that I wouldn't find out who you had been talking to. I never wanted to know. I just wanted to see your face, to check you were all right. Every night I would check you when you were asleep, rest my hand on your side and feel the steady rhythm of your breathing, stroke your hair gently away from your face and kiss you. Most times you would roll over towards me, one of your arms swinging round like the yardarm on a sailing boat, the back of your hand catching me in the mouth or smashing into my ear. I probably shouldn't say this but I quite liked being beaten up by you. You punched pretty hard and if you didn't make a satisfying contact you would hit me again until you did.

I've got to go and get Robbie now. Please come with me. I'll be waiting by the door.

I love you.

Daddy

7

Hello, my sweetheart,

It has been and continues to be a difficult day. Every day is difficult. Mummy has withdrawn and only speaks when I ask her something or if she is called to the telephone. Robbie spent most of the day in Newport again. I hope and I feel that he gets greater comfort from being with his friends. He is meant to go back to school tomorrow but he hates the idea. He also hates the thought of staying at home. He has missed his mock GCSEs and says that he cannot do the coursework. I will help him as best I can. Perhaps when he goes back, the routine and the surface normality will help him. I am more worried about Mummy.

I have to go to London tomorrow for Uncle Davy to pick up a load of olive oil from the Fresh Olive Company. The last time I went you came with me. I think it was the time we stopped at that weird McDonald's in Neasden, the one that looks like a converted town hall. We were in the big black van, Davy's pride and joy, and I smashed it into a bollard trying to turn the corner into the 'drive thru'. You couldn't stop laughing and I begged you not to tell anybody except that you told Simy the moment we got back to the factory. I remember Simy grinning, so pleased that somebody else other than him had put a dent in one of the works vans. 'Bollarded the van, eh?' he said. I've never heard anybody so cheerful following an accident. You just cackled and called me an arsehole.

Horsey went to play with Jonny [Farr] today. Suzanne brought him back about half an hour ago. He is getting his books together for tomorrow and watching *Futurama* at the same time. It's the one where Bender gets a sex change so that he can win the female robot Olympics. Not one of my favourites.

It has rained for most of the day, a horrible grey drizzle. The sort of day even you struggled to enjoy although you would have found something good to say about it. Mummy and I went to Bishop's Stortford to buy Horsey some new school trousers. We ended up buying about forty pairs of socks and a similar number of boys' boxer shorts. Auntie Jill bought Robbie some boxer shorts for Christmas but he said they were no good because of some mysterious chafing he discovered just below the waist. I find the whole thing very sinister.

The Reverend Titford – you don't know him, but he looked after your service – e-mailed us today. I can't really tell you about it yet. People keep ringing up and saying how beautiful the service was. How can it have been beautiful? It would have been beautiful if you had been standing next to me, twisting my thumb in your iron grip or whispering something naughty about Auntie Trish. I can't remember it. I can't remember what I said. I can remember your wonderful poem which you read at Dan's funeral, me standing behind you as you stood so tall and proud before the lectern, more than 700 people hanging on your every word. A twelve-year-old girl with a voice so clear and strong that not a single word was lost. You said that you could tell a person by their friends and that Dan had such wonderful friends. You have the most wonderful friends. There are some things I can't talk about yet but I want to tell you about Robbie and the kids from school. You would love them so much. I will screw my courage to the sticking place, an old quote from *Macbeth* that you heard me say on several occasions and always told me to 'shut it'. Still, it seems apt now.

Believe it or not, I've got to go and get Robbie again. I know you will come with me. Unfortunately the football is on the radio and I'm putting it on whether you like it or not.

I love you so much.

Daddy

Oh my darling,

I stare at your face on my computer and I cannot believe that you are not in the next room. My life, our life, has become a dream, a surreal nightmare from which we may never awake. The last few days have somehow been even worse. You are everywhere. In every thought, in every shop, waiting for me around every corner. Today I went shopping for food at the Waitrose in Bishop's Stortford. I saw you running to the olive counter and found myself staring vacantly at bowls of mixed olives, sun-blushed tomatoes, strange, inedible pasta salads that you didn't like either. Whom would I buy them for? I walked straight past all the vegetables. No bags of green salad or your favourite Caesar salad. Robbie and Horsey hate vegetables and Mummy will only eat soup. I have no desire to make anything healthy for myself. I have taken to eating Tesco or Waitrose ready-made Indian meals. Yesterday I had a terrible stomach all day. It didn't seem worth mentioning.

I didn't write yesterday. I went to London just as I told you I would. Uncle Davy said I could go in the car because there wasn't much to pick up. Robbie stayed with Mummy. He only went back to school today. At least I think he went to school. I dropped him off outside Gary's house just as we used to. I watched him walk off vaguely in the right direction. He is with Cheese as he always is now. She comforts him and distracts him so I think it must be a good thing. I like her very much. You had good taste.

The London trip was difficult. I drove to all the places we used to go to together. I put the heating up to five but I was still cold and found myself listening to gibberish on the radio, simply not to feel alone. I am beginning to get angry. I didn't really feel angry before. I can't properly describe how I feel. Lonely, bewildered. Sometimes the physical act of longing is so strong that it is unbearable. The worst times come with unbidden thoughts about what actually happened. They come most often just as I am falling asleep. A physical jolt like an electric shock passes through me and only by force of will am I able to banish images from my mind. I get up and go into the kitchen and roll a cigarette and stare at pictures of you.

There's not really much to tell about going to London. It rained again all day and I forgot to tax the car so if I had been stopped I would have been banned. I already have too many points on my licence. I didn't feel like chatting with the guys at Fresh Olive or that weird Products from Spain place. They wouldn't let me in. I had to ring up and tell them I was standing outside the door. A woman with a strangled Spanish accent told me to press the button.

'I've been pressing the button,' I told her.

'Prez eet agin,' she said.

So I prezzed it. Eventually a surly Spanish bloke opened the door. I don't think he was Spanish at all, just pretending to be Spanish to allow him to be extra surly. He wouldn't have been surly to you. I didn't stop at the Neasden McDonald's but I bought an egg and bacon sandwich from a petrol station in Hendon. It was horrible and probably poisonous.

I have decided that I might sue the railway company. The station must be made safer. I know you wouldn't normally be interested but I'm going to tell you anyway. If I don't do something they'll just carry on as before until something else terrible happens. Trust me on this one. I know you think I'm being silly or showing off but I'm not. I won't give up, not ever.

Mrs Wiggett came round to see Mummy this afternoon. She brought a huge new bag with her. She calls it her shoplifting bag because it would be perfect if she ever decided to embark upon a life of crime. She works as assistant manager in the Cancer Research shop in Saffron Walden. I don't know why she left Country Casuals. She is very vague about it. I wonder if it has anything to do with her shoplifting bag. She has been a wonderful friend to us. So has Alan although he appears to have grown even taller, which is odd for a man of forty-three. He comes round with Tom and stands in the kitchen. We talk about football mainly. It is lucky I'm such an expert.

Horsey is getting excited about his birthday, which is on Sunday as you know. He hasn't actually asked for anything but I'm going to get him an XBOX 360 which is some new-fangled computer games console. It's more real than real life. If only that were true.

Each day, each moment brings another memory. Or the same memory. I have no bad memories except for the last one. Do you remember that time we walked across the water meadows behind the Mill Hotel in Sudbury just after we had finished our delivery round? We bumped into Jane Hyde Parker walking her dog. You made me walk across the water pipe next to the bridge and I fell and scraped all the skin off my inner thigh. They could hear you cackling in Long Melford. Then we played at jumping over those small, tributary-like streams that crossed the field. I can't believe that I was a better jumper than you. I think you were wearing new trainers. They weren't new after you landed ankle-deep in a bog. I did my back in as usual, not that you cared. Which reminds me of the time we went rowing at Dedham. Just you, me and Horsey. Mummy hates boats and water as you well know and Robbie is too lazy to row. I rowed us perfectly about half a mile downstream and then my back went. I couldn't move. You and Horsey had to row us back, which you did brilliantly. It wasn't that long ago that we went back to Dedham to see whether I could revive my old injury. I can see you now, rowing us viciously into the bank. Your rowing skills had waned somewhat. Still, you knew I was there so you didn't have to try. I can't really go on now. That last time in Dedham was such a short while ago. I need a roll-up.

I love you, darling.

Daddy

Hello, poppet,

Bad day today. I can't get horrible images out of my head. I keep crying. The Reverend came round, the one I told you about. He is an extremely nice man. He came at lunchtime while I was in Saffron Walden buying some ludicrously expensive truffles for a hamper order. Mummy was sitting on that really cheap settee we bought from Homebase and somehow got in the back of the Zafira. The Reverend Richard was on the other settee. Nobody was talking when I came in. I sat down next to Mummy and the silence carried on for about another five minutes. I realised eventually that we were meant to talk to him. Like a psychiatrist. They don't actually say anything, they just listen. Great job. It's too late now but I reckon I would have been brilliant. Mummy, I don't think, had said anything at all.

I told him that I couldn't make any sense of my feelings. I don't think I'll ever believe that you have gone. I used to dream that life was a dream and that eventually everyone would wake up to find that they didn't exist. That nothing existed. For me the enormity of what has happened is just too terrible to grasp. I am like a zombie. Sometimes I feel quite normal. For the rest I am in hell.

I read in the paper that every day 3,000 children die from malaria. That's not including the victims of AIDS, natural disasters, murder, terrorism, accidents. I told the Reverend that I found myself thinking all the time about all the other grieving parents, that I could draw some kind of strength from not being alone. Then I felt intensely selfish. That I should be somehow glad that others were suffering too. He nodded wisely. 'You are quite normal,' he said. When he left he hugged Mummy and shook my hand although he tried to hug me too. I've gone off being hugged. He told us that we were brave. I don't see we have any choice. We owe our lives to Robbie and Horsey. They deserve the best chance.

I can't believe that only five weeks ago our lives were normal. You would be sitting at my desk. Robbie would be upstairs disappearing in a cloud of cigarette smoke. You lied for him, I know you did, when you said he didn't smoke. He doesn't even try to hide it now and I am disposed to be lenient. In five years it will be illegal to smoke anyway and that's not enough time to do any lasting damage. Moreover I won't give him any money for cigarettes so he has to beg, borrow and steal from his mates. I used to have a mate called Micky Turton who smoked twenty Rothmans before breakfast. That's serious smoking. One Rothmans is enough to bring a grown man to his knees.

Sometimes the reality slaps me in the face and I feel almost unable to breathe. Not sick. It's like a panic attack. I don't know what to do. I don't suppose I'll ever know what to do.

Today has been ghastly. I need to collate all the
newspaper reports for the lawyers and Paul is going to
the station to photograph every angle of the track, the
platform, the ticket office, the crossing point. I can't go
to the station. I went twice. The first time was on the
Tuesday afterwards. I haven't told you about this before
although I hope you know anyway. Robbie and the
band played an impromptu concert at the station after
school. They played 'Time of Your Life' because it was
your favourite song. Robbie, Dean, Chitson and a guy
called Matt, who has already left school, played guitar
and James and Charlie McPartland and Sam, and several
other boys who I don't know very well, sang. It was
raining and dark and they sat on the pavement outside
the station. The white picket fence behind them was a
wall of flowers and pictures and letters. Poems pinned to
fence posts and pictures of you and Livvy. Over 200
kids turned up and some parents. We were there and
Livvy's parents. Murray came from London and stood at
the back, and the Wiggetts and the Danes, and Jonny
and Suzanne. Auntie Jill was there with Olly, Toby and
Patrick, and Oma was there, frail but upright, supported
by Uncle Davy and Auntie Trish. Even Simy came with
Emma. There were so many people that the police
arrived to cordon off the road and a chaplain came from
the rail company.

When Robbie started playing nobody made a sound.
The children made a path for us through the crowd so
that we could stand at the front and afterwards the
children came to hug us, all of them, kids I'd never met

17

before. I will go on. I will tell you more but I can't at the moment. Just know that Robbie loves you. He has always loved you.

Bless you, my darling.

Daddy

My sweetheart,

It's Saturday 7 January, the day before Horsey's birthday. We used to love Saturday nights, watching crap television, snuggled under duvets in the living room. What a diet of indigestible television. *Strictly Come Dancing* followed by the end of *Pop Idol*. Now we've got *Celebrity Big Brother*. It could be the most horrible thing ever to befoul a television screen. You would love it.

Paul and Mel are on their way round. They said they are not going to stay long. Mummy has been asleep on the green sofa bed in the study/dining room. John Keeling is coming round as well. You don't know John. He was the best man at our wedding. I worked with him at Warner's in the eighties. We've been friends for twenty-two years apparently. He has been amazing this last month. He has come whenever he has been able and his determination to be happy and tell jokes is nothing short of remarkable. He wishes he had known you. Perhaps he will get to know you through our stories and pictures and the huge part of our lives that you always will be.

We went to Sudbury earlier to buy Horsey his birthday present. It's a PSP, a hand-held playstation. I can't afford it but as I've never been able to afford anything I don't see what difference it makes. Anyway Paul has persuaded me that the MBNA credit card has more than enough money to pay for Horsey's playstation. He jokes that MBNA stands for the Military Bank of Northern Albania. As Albania doesn't appear to have an army, it might as well spend its money on us. Paul is full of this kind of wisdom but you knew that already, didn't you?

Last night Mummy talked to me for the first time. We were sitting in the kitchen. It was past midnight and neither of us were speaking. I was holding Mummy's hand and she was just gazing at the picture of you, the one that Paul took in Brighton in the summer. At least I think it was summer. The rain was relentless and the wind was roaring along the seafront. Your hair is literally dancing and your mouth is wide open, your eyes sparkling. It is a picture of pure happiness. Only you could be happy in a storm on Brighton beach. I wasn't there. It was the day I took Robbie and Cheese to Reading. I came for you later and we went to Reading together.

Mummy cries silently. She always has. She never made a sound when you were born. Not like all the other women in the ward who were screaming like banshees. Mummy suffers in terrible silence. She stroked your picture and turned to me. 'There are pockets,' she said. 'Pockets of time when I can bear it. Watching television for a little while or a conversation. The rest of the time is madness.'

I said that we have a purpose. We have to make sure that Robbie and Horsey grow up to live full lives. They have a right to be happy. They mustn't grow up in an atmosphere of misery. Maybe we should try to live worthwhile lives, not spend years pursuing useless dreams of making money so that we can live in a big house and go out a lot and wear expensive clothes and go on loads of holidays. As if that really makes anybody happy. But what really matters is that you are not gone. Your soul, the thing that made you you, is indestructible. You can't destroy energy.

I want to believe that this life is just a stage in some kind of constant evolution. Why would nature make human beings so frail, so prone to illness, so incapable of defending themselves in a physical sense? The only thing we have going for us is our brains. Our ability to reason. No other creature, as far as we know, has any concept of its own mortality. No other creature leaves things for the next generation to learn from. Our whole existence serves only one purpose: a constant search for knowledge. Why, unless this life is just a preparation for the next journey? I have always instinctively believed in the soul for want of a better word. A soul cannot be destroyed. I want to believe that you are free now to explore the universe, to sense and feel things beyond our comprehension, to float amongst the stars. I know you are not gone. What is the point of thinking otherwise? Why take the view that we are just here for this infinitesimally small amount of time and then we cease to be?

Why do we have such horrible words for the business of dying? Death. Funeral. Undertaker. Cemetery. Cold, cruel words. I will not let you go. I will not accept that you have ceased to be. People tell me that I will always have you inside me. They don't understand. I am not crying for myself. I am crying for you. But I want to know that you have gone on to something better. Sometimes, like now, I believe that.

It's late and I am a bit drunk. Paul and Mel left about two hours ago but Mrs Wiggett turned up and John is standing outside smoking dope. Don't be shocked, he's forty-six. He can smoke some dope if he wants. We played a Trivial Pursuit pop quiz for an hour. I don't think you would have been able to bear it. I can hear them coughing outside. I don't want to leave you but I'm so tired.

Do you want to know a secret? I love you.

Daddy

Hello, my darling,

I'm sorry I didn't write yesterday. It was Horsey's birthday and the day just disappeared. I kept meaning to come and talk to you but every time one set of people left, more arrived. We didn't get up until midday anyway. Suzanne brought Jonny round who is beginning to resemble his father more and more. He looks like a friendly dalek. We decided to go up to the Swan for lunch. Mummy invited Paul and Mel and Miles, and Robbie took Cheese. The last time we ate in the Swan we were all together. You and Horsey spent the whole time asking me for money so you could play that infernal *Who Wants to be a Millionaire* game. I sat at the head of the table so all I could do was look down it and see that you weren't there. I forced down one of the Swan's speciality school-dinner-style roasts while Paul and Mel ate a bowl of chips. I approve of them as dinner guests. They are remarkably cheap. No sooner had the children finished their food than they wanted to go home so I gave Robbie the keys and told him to keep an eye on Horsey crossing the road. We so-called adults stayed on for an hour or so and then we walked over to the church and lit all the candles for you. There was nobody else in the church

except for a small, busy woman with unfeasibly loud
shoes. She clattered about, turning all the lights on, and
then asked us to leave as she was about to lock up. I
wondered why she had turned all the lights on. Maybe it's
a *Catch-22*-type thing. Perhaps the vicar only gives a
sermon when the church is empty.

When we got home Paul and Mel and Miles prepared
to leave but no sooner had they gone than Terry and
Sylvie James turned up with Frank. I was so tired but
there seemed to be no escape. Terry staggered in with a
whole crate of red wine, twelve bottles of red Merlot.

'This should keep you going for a while,' he boomed.

'You can't give us that,' I said. 'It's absurd. We're not
wholesalers.'

Terry wouldn't hear of it. Still, we managed to drink
three bottles before they finally left at about midnight.
Sylvie talked to Mummy. She's like the newsdesk for the
Sunday People. That's a newspaper that devotes most of its
pages to what's happening in *Big Brother* or grotesque
stories about babies born with two heads. I like Terry. He
may be the biggest person I know but he is very gentle
and very generous. He really cares. Sometimes, like when
I'm talking to Terry, telling him about how you came to
work with me at Uncle Davy's factory and how you
would carry everything, no matter how heavy, and you
would take on any job and do it better than most, if not
all, of the adults, I can only smile. It was such a short time
ago. I cannot believe that you will not be getting up with
me on Saturday morning, bleary-eyed and bolshie as hell,
but wonderful company. Or you would be, certainly by

the time we made it to the McDonald's in Braintree where you demanded breakfast: a large portion of chips and an orange juice.

Do you remember the time I succumbed to a sausage and egg McMuffin? I had eaten perhaps two mouthfuls and you asked for a bite. I've never known anyone so enthusiastic about any kind of foodstuff from McDonald's. 'That's delicious,' you said, your eyes flashing. I knew what was coming next. 'Can you go back and get me one?' We'd only driven about three miles so I turned round and drove back to buy you your own personal sausage and egg McMuffin. As we turned around again to make our second attempt at completing our journey, I enjoyed some rare silence while you embarked upon your second breakfast. I think you ate half before depositing what was left on the dashboard. You were strangely silent. I looked over at you.

'Is it OK?' I said.

'It's the most disgusting thing I've ever eaten,' you said and then managed to make me feel guilty for buying it for you. Then you threw the remains out of the window. Before I had a chance to say anything, you informed me, thumb firmly in your mouth, that it was 'biodegradable'. I was too tired to be annoyed. Anyway after about a minute you took my hand and told me, as you so often did, that you loved me.

Terry was great last night. He is another who believes in the 'soul'. He says he is regularly visited by Sylvie's mum who hides his hairbrush because he hasn't got any hair so what does he need it for anyway. 'That's right, dear,' says

Sylvie, expert at listening to two conversations at once and commenting on both at exactly the right time. I fear our friendship has been rekindled to the point where we may have to go on holiday with them again. Terry is still the karaoke king. Do you remember that night in the bar in Menorca, sitting with Terry and Sylvie and all their mates, and they were trying to persuade the two of us to do a duet? We decided upon 'American Pic' but you bottled out of it at the last minute. I never really thanked you for that. It didn't save me from having to sing 'You've Lost That Loving Feeling' with Terry though.

Anyway, the real reason I didn't write yesterday was that by the time Terry and Sylvie left I was too tired to do anything. We made up all the beds in the living room as usual. Robbie sleeps on the red settee and Horsey sleeps on the cream number from Homebase. Mummy and I drag down Horsey's mattress from upstairs and sleep wedged between the two. At least we are all together. Nobody wants to go to a bedroom alone and I find it difficult to go upstairs at all. The door of your room is open at the end of the corridor and although I want to close it, I can't. Still, nothing has been moved in your room. Your dirty clothes are strewn all over the floor and on that uncomfortable pink chair in the corner. I haven't even turned your record player off.

Today has been worse than yesterday. Horsey didn't go to school. He just burst into tears this morning so we let him go back to bed or back to lying on the settee anyway.

★   ★   ★

I've just got back from picking Robbie up from Newport. He had dinner at Cheese's house, which was lucky for him because we haven't got any food. He's in quite a good mood. His teachers have told him that he can do his mock GCSEs at home. Maybe they'll let him do his real GCSEs at home too.

I went to Sudbury this morning to see Uncle Davy. I left Mummy with Horsey. I think they both slept until at least 1 p.m. I can't really describe how I feel when I'm alone. I can't believe what has happened although I know it has. It is unbearable. I cry and then I stop crying because it is pointless. An explosion of expanding emptiness and the worst thing is that I know there is nothing I can do. I turned on the car radio. On the news another family has lost a child. A boy of fourteen killed by a car while he was out on his bicycle. Just like you, he had done nothing wrong, just been in the wrong place at the wrong time. Knowing we are not alone doesn't make the pain go away. Nothing will ever make the pain go away.

I wasn't going to write any more tonight but I can't keep away from the computer. I have to keep talking and actually talking aloud doesn't work. I've set the beds up as usual. Horsey is almost asleep and Robbie has disappeared up to his room, probably for a quick fag. I just sat with Mummy at the kitchen table. We sit holding hands, not speaking. After all, what is there to say? Nothing we can say will make any difference. You made everybody happy.

Even people you only met once. I won't let anybody forget you. You made me so happy. Sometimes I realise that nothing can take that happiness away.

They held a special service for you and Livvy at Newport church and I had to speak. I didn't know what to say. I thought about it the night before and then I stopped. I would say whatever came into my mind at the time, vaguely hoping that something would. I really didn't want to think about it at all. I can't look upon anything that makes this real. So the next morning before the service I got up and started to put on my suit, the one you didn't like because the trousers don't fit properly, and then I thought that you wouldn't want me to wear a suit, so I put on a pair of a jeans and a white shirt and, in a moment of inspiration, your school tie, which was covered in suspicious stains and has a green merit badge stuck on the back, for physics of all things. I thought you were rubbish at physics. I couldn't do the tie up properly because of my fat neck. It was only then that I thought of something to say.

The sun shone so brightly that morning. John Keeling arrived at about 9.30 and by 10 Paul and Mel and Oma and a host of others were crammed into the kitchen. Murray came with Boyce and an old friend of mine called Nigel Flude who used to work at Polygram. Jules came, do you remember her? and Michelle, Stu's old girlfriend, and, of course, Stu himself, looking about 180 years old with a huge, grey beard and a walking stick. He can't really walk any more. Mummy seemed all right, distracted by so many people, and because it was a memorial service, it somehow wasn't as daunting. Dick Farr held the service and they think there were more than 800 people in the church. They even put speakers outside so that people who couldn't get in could still hear.

Livvy's father spoke first. Did you ever meet him? He seems a nice man but quite controlled. We sat in the front row of pews with Paul and Mel and Oma and Olly. Cheese and Robbie sat on the end. Horsey sat behind us with Auntie Jill and Patrick and Toby. Eventually I had to speak. I still had no idea what to say. What can you say? My shirt was hanging out and the tie was loose with my collar undone. I apologised for my appearance and asked Mr Priestley, the headmaster, who was sitting very close to the front, not to give me a detention. It was cheap but I got a laugh. I didn't say much. I felt that if I started I would never stop. I could talk about you every minute for a hundred years and never repeat myself. Robbie played 'Time of Your Life' with the rest of the band. I held Mummy and Oma, who stood one on either side of me, and together we sang the words from a Green Day song in that beautiful church with the sun streaming through the stained-glass windows.

Afterwards we went to the pub, the Coach and Horses, and told stories about you until the sun finally set and the darkness drew us home.

Each day becomes more difficult. We long for you and that part of us that knows you will never come helps us to sit down and stare into the void. What if? What if you had come to work with me on that day? What if you and Livvy had decided to go by bus? What if? What if? What if? I have to push the 'whys' and the 'what ifs' away otherwise I will go mad.

Goodnight, my darling. Please come and see me? I am waiting.

Bless you.

Daddy

Hello, my angel,

Sorry I didn't write yesterday. I couldn't. I am like a man waking up from a coma and each day brings reality a little closer. I went to Cambridge to buy a DVD for a hamper order. It's the first time I have been to Cambridge without you. I parked in Lion Yard and walked, head down, to the HMV shop. I couldn't look up, couldn't look anybody in the eye. There seemed to be girls of your age everywhere. Smiling, talking, on bicycles, all with a lifetime of possibilities ahead of them. I couldn't bear it. I rang Oma because Mummy had gone with Mel Bowe to the Real Life centre for people with learning disabilities where Mel works. Mummy may start working with Mel.

Oma told me that there is a purpose. That you are out there. That we have to believe. I hate the West, our lack of spiritualism. We worship money, success, superficiality. We are completely unprepared to cope with unexpected death. Eventually I got myself together enough to buy the film I needed and then I made my way home. I think about you all the time. Even when I'm trying to do something else, I think about you. Yesterday was a day in hell. Every day is a day in hell.

Today has been a little better. Adele, Bee's mother,

rang, and asked if she could come round. Mummy has resisted until now. I suppose because you and Bee had fallen out. Neither of us had any idea why, and you always refused to tell us, but Mummy said yes to Adele and she turned up just before twelve. She stayed for nearly three hours and we are both glad that she came. She brought a poem that you had written for Bee which we had never seen before. It is utterly beautiful. That you could write something so passionate, so vivid for your friend and not show us – but then why would you? You had forever to show us whatever pleased you. Adele said you wrote the poem after going on holiday with them to Cornwall. She was so funny. Your extraordinary gift for making people feel as if you had known them all your life after meeting them for less than five minutes. Apparently you called Adele's mother Nan. Well, I suppose somebody had to. You left your glow on everybody you met. Here is your poem, just in case you have forgotten it:

In the Wilderness

The wilderness down by Croakendale Lane
Across tigerlily ponds, is an enchanted place
Where giant oaks gather together
It's dark and black and mysterious no matter what the
    weather
Brown toads hidden under bark and moss
Tell you weird riddles so you're sure to get lost
Toadstool mushrooms deadly and poisonous
Look strangely inviting, like they want you to eat them

Huge dragonflies of emerald green
Black owls with yellow eyes that have never been seen
Rats with red tails and purple eyes
Watch from hidden dens as you walk slowly by
Hundreds of bluebells dripping with dew
Growing in perfect circles
That seems odd to me and you
But the strangest things of all are these beautiful little
　　creatures
Like faeries that fly
They're pretty like ballerinas
Named after all sorts of flowers and plants
They stare at you with tiny beady eyes that seem to
　　enchant
There is always a dreaming, bewitching aroma
Drifting through the air
Everywhere you look something dark seems to stare
Strange, beautiful flowers growing by rippling streams
Different coloured lights shining in beams
Waterfalls of dreams and nightmares falling from the
Tree tops
Splashes of enchanting water, the smell of juicy berries
Never stops
Watch out for the twisting branches winding around
　　your
Feet
You can't stay there too long, you can never fall asleep
So when you walk down Croakendale Lane, remember
　　to
Catch the number 963 bus

Otherwise you'll find yourself wandering into the
wilderness.

By Charlie Thompson
written for Beth E. Meader

Thank you, Charlie, for everything. I want to walk down
Croakendale Lane with Mummy. Maybe Robbie and
Horsey will come too. I know you will be there.

Adele talked about her sister Rebecca, Auntie Becka to
you. She lives in South Africa near Johannesburg and she
has had her baby. Adele says that Rebecca has always lived
like a nomad, never wanting anything material. Not long
ago all she owned was a pair of shoes. She lost her best
friend when she was fourteen and it changed her life.
Now the same thing has happened to Beth. Life is so
strange. Adele said that when Beth found out about what
had happened she just started screaming. I'm going to try
to keep on writing. I want to cry but I am trying not to.
I want to tell you about some more things.

We're not very good at death round here. We're not
prepared. In Africa death is commonplace. Families have
lots of children because they know half of them will die.

Beth's Auntie Becka made friends with a little African
boy a few years ago. Adele couldn't remember his name.
She thinks he was about twelve. Becka went to find him
last year but when she got to the village and asked after
him, she was told that he was 'with God now'. Perhaps he
is with you. Perhaps the fact that you both knew Becka
will bring you together.

Mrs Wiggett has just arrived. It's eight o'clock and soon I must make the pilgrimage to Newport to pick up Robbie. Mrs Wiggett will keep Mummy company until I get back.

Adele talked about Christopher. So many people hide their own catastrophes just below the surface. You know how severely disabled he is. He will never be able to get a job or feed himself, or, most distressingly of all, talk. Adele says that her own grief comes in cycles. This morning she woke up having had a dream in which Christopher could talk. The realisation that it had been only a dream completely destroyed her day. She said his disablement sometimes feels as if she has never really had a son at all. A kind of living bereavement. But soon she was laughing, recounting a story of how, once when you had stayed the night, she found you in his bed, cuddling him in the morning. Beth was still fast asleep in her room. You and Christopher were both hiding under the sheets. You poked your head out and said, 'It's really wet under here,' before disappearing under the sheet again. Adele told you that it was dribble. Christopher dribbles a lot, especially in his sleep. Your head popped out for a second look. 'Good,' you said. 'I thought it was wee.'

Only you, Charlie. Only you.

No sooner had Adele left than Di Nicholson arrived with the most spectacular bunch of white roses. James, her eldest son, who is Robbie's age, has chosen you as a subject for his GCSE English essay. She is another whose quiet friendship has been as welcome as it has been unexpected. Although this is her fourth visit and I have never felt comfortable enough to call her anything but Mrs Nicholson. She too has a hidden history of tragedy. Her sister lost her grandchild in a car accident when he was only nine and just last year another sister's son killed himself. He was only forty. Strangely the little boy was killed in Africa. Di was there when it happened. She said the local women wailed for four whole days, only stopping to eat and sleep. After four days, life resumed a kind of normality and the family had somehow found a sort of peace. I wish I could wail.

Robbie Gladwell called. We are going to see him on Friday. He says he has lots to tell us.

I love you so much. You are my darling Charlikins. Bless you.

Daddy

Charlie,

I don't know that I can go on much longer without you. The grief has come in waves today as if I am standing waist deep in a rough sea, the constant swell smashing into me, knocking me down and each time it is harder to get up.

Mummy went on a course this morning at Wicken House. She didn't want to go but Susannah, one of the teachers from her school, arrived at nine and wouldn't leave until Mummy went with her. I had never met Susannah before but she has been to see us three times at least. People say to us that they will do anything, absolutely anything, to help and the extraordinary thing is that they mean it, even people we hardly know. In the midst of misery, the very best of people shines through. Will Holt's mother rang to offer to do the shopping. Did you ever meet Will Holt's mother? Her name is Diane and she comes from a place called Eight Mile in Detroit where Eminem comes from. She looks like Janis Joplin, a famous American singer who died about thirty years ago. She made us a lasagne before Christmas that must have been from one of Eminem's own recipes. I ate it all the same.

While Mummy was on her course I went to Sudbury to see Oma. She has press cuttings from the accident, which I need to send on to the lawyer. I made the mistake of reading one of them. I have managed to avoid all the articles concerning the accident until now. I cannot get out of my head how only a second can make the difference between life and death. One second earlier and you would be with me now or I would be in the kitchen and you would be on MSN. Life would be normal. Tomorrow might be a day to look forward to. How could I have saved you? I see you so vividly, laughing, smiling, with a thousand different thoughts running through your wonderful head. I start screaming but you can't hear me. Why can't you hear me? I don't know what I'm talking about. I'm sorry.

I can hear Mummy putting some washing on the radiator in the hall, probably school shirts for Horsey and Robbie for the morning. The house is so quiet. Horsey is playing on the PSP I bought him for his birthday. Robbie is in Newport with Cheese. You should be here. It is half past five. By now you would have started eating in between fighting with Horsey. Mummy would be pleading with you both to stop it and Horsey would be doing his trick crying act to get you into trouble. Perhaps you would be making yourself a salad in one of those deep white bowls that you could rest perfectly in your lap whilst watching *The Simpsons*. Although it probably wouldn't be *The Simpsons* unless Horsey got his way because you preferred those ghastly girlie programmes like *America's Next Top Model* or *The Tyra Banks Show*. How could you watch that stuff? I swear you did it on purpose just to annoy me.

While I'm writing to you like this, you are with me. I can see you, feel you near me, almost pretend that nothing has happened. The house is so quiet though. I have to turn the volume up in my head.

Darling,

I don't know what happened last time. Something distracted me and I didn't get back. Each day is getting worse now. It's impossible to imagine feeling more desperate but the next morning is even blacker and emptier. Mummy is sinking and I am trying to hold on to her. She slept most of the day today and then at about five we went over to see Liam's mother, Andrea, at James and Dean's house in Stansted. We've just got back. James and Dean's mum is really nice and really short. Andrea hugged Mummy for such a long time, cradling her head into her shoulder. We were all crying and not talking. James tried to amuse us by trying on his mother's clothes, which was extremely odd. Robbie and Liam played guitar and Horsey found a computer game so he was happy. For dinner we had chips and pretzels and I drank four giant cups of tea. In between we watched a new programme that you would love, called *Dancing on Ice*. The same as *Strictly Come Dancing* except on ice. It was rubbish actually because nobody could do it plus the fact that the so-called celebrities were a bunch of actors who once had a walk-on part in *Coronation Street*.

I know I'm trying to be funny but it is such an effort. I am writing because it makes me think of you as if you are just in a foreign country or away at University. If I keep writing for long enough, you'll come home.

Mummy just came into the study or the room where the computer is or whatever you want to call it. She sat on that green bed settee thing which is several feet deep in duvets. She had a cigarette and she kind of perched on top of the duvets because she is too light to sink into them.

It is past midnight now and Mummy has finally gone to lie down in the sitting room. I managed to get her to take a diazepam, which is a sleeping pill, but double strength. With luck she won't dream. We moved back to the kitchen and Mummy talked, not really to me but to you. She wants you to come for her. I held her hand but she didn't seem to be aware of me. She said I could look after Robbie and Horsey. I feel as if a monster is staring at me from the side and if I look at it I will sink too. I stare straight ahead, not looking to the side, not looking down, trying to hold on to Mummy. I can't get the image of the *Titanic* out of my head, but I'm the one floating on the driftwood and Mummy is in the water. She keeps telling me to let her go because I am holding on to her but she wants to go, she wants to be with you. I can't let her go, Charlie, not ever. Mummy is wearing all your clothes, the jeans you drew on, a Frankenstein stitch on the thigh and a black top with a black, fake fur collar. She wears the

Ugg boots we bought in Cambridge last Christmas
because you used to wear them. She won't eat any more.
For a little while she ate. First it was only soup but then
she ate a potato and shortly after that an omelette. She's
gone two days without anything. I try to get her to eat
but she won't. I will go to the doctor on Monday but I
doubt it will do any good. I have looked on the internet.
There are sites for bereaved parents but they all seem the
same. They paraphrase what they are going to say to you
before they say it. The usual things. Time will teach you
to cope. The pain will never go away but you will learn
to live with it. Uncle Davy has already told me. He has
called Compassionate Friends a few times. I don't think it
has really helped him although the people mean well.
They must know what it's like. Except you were the best,
Charlie. You drew a picture on the world that nobody
could miss.

I'm going back to see Mummy now. Robbie is in his
bedroom with Cheese. Horsey is asleep, I think. I am
going to take a diazepam too. Tomorrow Uncle Stu is
coming. He's coming via air ambulance from Portugal, at
least that's what Mel Bowe reckons. He rings me two or
three times a day, almost always in tears to tell me which
records he has just been playing for you. He appears to
live in a bar with a jukebox full of seventies classics.
Today he was playing 'The Weight' by The Band. Not
one of your favourites partly because I don't think you
ever heard it. I always loved it though, and 'Tangled Up
in Blue' by Bob Dylan, which you did know although I
think you pretended to like it to keep me happy.

I will find you, Charlie, I promise. I will never stop looking.

Night–night, poppet. I'll talk again in the morning. Bless you.

Daddy

Sweetheart,

I didn't write yesterday. It was Sunday. Outside a
relentless drizzle fell from a grey sky. Inside misery and
hopelessness reigned. Mummy is drifting further away and
Robbie is on a knife edge. He, too, now seems to be
unable to cope, tears are always in his eyes. Horsey alone
shows real strength although he knows only too well what
is happening. I am becoming more and more desperate.
I am going to the doctor's in about half an hour. I don't
know what he will be able to do but maybe we need
some stronger pills. Anything to keep going. Suzanne
Darling has just arrived with a huge bag of cakes from the
baker's on the corner. I haven't been in there since.
I can't face the lady who always said, 'Can I get you
anything else?' in that high-pitched voice. I know she is a
nice lady but I can't think what to say to her. Mummy is
a wraith now. She moves slowly and speaks only when
spoken to, her voice is so soft that I can hardly hear her.
Last night she told me that when you died, she died too.
So, I think, did I.

I have been trying to work but no coherent thoughts
come. I will have to sell the house just to pay the bills and
then, perhaps, we will move to Newport so that Robbie

and Horsey can be near their friends and walk to school. We don't need much space.

We have fallen out with Oma. I wish we hadn't but Mummy cannot take any more and Oma doesn't understand. We are not soldiers. We can't just do what she tells us as if nothing had happened. She repeats the same mantra every day. 'The boys must work harder now.' 'Make sure Horsey practises his clarinet every day.' She accused us of living like gypsies. We've always lived like gypsies, that's how we live. I do love her and I know how she must be suffering too but I can't really take it at the moment. Just getting through each day is the most we can hope for. I am going to the doctor now. I will write more later.

I love you so much.

Daddy

Hi, darling,

The day got worse if that's possible. The school rang to say that there had been a fire and Robbie was the only one missing from the roll-call. Mummy collapsed. I just shut down. I rang him and rang him on his mobile, to find out eventually that he had gone to Cambridge to see Cheese without signing out or letting anybody know. He is still there now. I have to go to get him at midnight. I am not angry but he must tell us what he is doing. I am so frightened of the telephone. I hate telephones.

Paul and Mel Bowe have just arrived so I will have to stop again. The doctor gave us antidepressant tablets but they will take about ten days to work. Ten days. It might as well be ten years. I can't think further ahead than tomorrow. However, maybe they will help.

It is Robbie's birthday tomorrow. I went to Saffron Walden to buy him some presents and do some belated shopping. The streets were deserted by 5 p.m. and I walked down the middle of the road past W.H. Smith and Duffy Moons. I don't know where you came from but suddenly you were walking beside me. I could almost feel your arm linked through mine, pulling me in exactly the direction I didn't want to go. I could see you so clearly, still wearing the same thing. Light blue tracksuit bottoms and a pinkish T-shirt, your hair in a ponytail, bouncing as you walked. You said, 'I love you, Pupps,' just like always.

Uncle Davy says that Dan comes to him and lifts him but I knew you weren't really there, that you were in my mind, and it was somehow worse than not seeing you at all. In the car on the way home I thought about how vivid you had been and perhaps, some day, I will be grateful for such visions. Now I can only remember when it was really you. I can still feel you, the softness of your skin, your strength, your beautiful, irreplaceable voice.

I rang up Compassionate Friends this morning. It is a helpline for people like us staffed by other bereaved parents. I spoke to a gentle woman called Pam who lost her son five years ago. She was very nice but, ultimately, I wish that I hadn't rung. She told me she didn't believe in the spirit. When you die, you die and that's it. I can't believe that. I know your spirit is out there. John Keeling says that it is impossible to destroy electricity and that is essentially what powers us. You exist somewhere, I know you do, and I will see you again.

I must go. Paul and Mel don't deserve to sit in silence with Mummy although I will not be much better company.

Sleep well, my angel.

I love you.

Daddy

It's a quarter past eleven and I've got to go and fetch Robbie in about fifteen minutes. Paul and Mel have just left. Paul made us laugh because he went to see his doctor, who is so old and bent over that he can only examine people's shoes. Paul was hilarious.

'What appears to be the matter with your shoes then, my boy?'

'Nothing,' said Paul, 'my ears are blocked.'

'What?' said the doctor. 'You'll have to speak up.'

I'm going to put my shoes on now. I know you would be asking to come with me if you were awake. If not, you would want to know in the morning why I hadn't woken you up to take you. Robbie is in a great deal of pain. Mummy says he is taking it out on us because he has no one else to take it out on. He is very short with me and bursts into tears at the slightest thing. All I want to do is help him. We are all learning how to behave with each other. We have all had to start again. Our old life is over for ever. Our new life has begun. I do not hold out much hope for Mummy or myself but Robbie and

Horsey must be all right. Everything we do must be for them. It's half past eleven now. I have to go.

Bless you. I hope you will be with me.

I love you. Night-night.

Daddy

Hi, darling,

It's half past one in the morning. Mummy and Robbie are in the kitchen talking. Horsey is asleep in the sitting room. There is school tomorrow but it doesn't matter. Robbie is talking. We spoke in the car on the way home and then for about half an hour just sitting outside the house. He says he can't see the point in his exams. Why learn long division and trigonometry when you'll probably go through your whole life and never ever say the words, let alone use the skill? I know there are things I could have said. Boring, grown-up things, but, for once, I managed to keep my mouth shut and just let him talk. He wondered how anything else could matter any more. I told him his music matters. He's so good, Charlie. He plays for us sometimes and it makes us cry. He says he's lonely. We are all lonely. We'll always be lonely. And as usual Robbie found the right word. All this time, all I really feel is lonely without you.

I was in the kitchen smoking a last cigarette and you were there, in my mind, at Reading in the summer. I was walking behind you, watching you and Cheese, your new best friend, arms looped around each other's waists, talking and laughing, another older sister for you to torment. I was so happy that you and she became friends. Robbie

was with his mates doing all sorts of hideous things I'd
have been better off not knowing about. Then as night
fell and the others eventually went off to watch some
band we'd never heard of, you and I were together alone,
sitting about ten feet away from the beer tent on a pile of
rubbish and you saw someone light a fire and you asked
whether we could light a fire too and I was all middle-
aged worry that somebody would come and tell us off but
how could I say no to you? So we gathered all the
rubbish we could find and built this huge tower of crap
and then you set fire to it all with my lighter. It was the
biggest and best fire and soon fires sprang up everywhere.
Your face is glowing in the firelight. I can see it now.
Beaming with pleasure. We found every dirty cup and
filthy plate there was to find and threw them on the
inferno. People came to warm their hands or just squat
and talk and there you were, thirteen years old, with
punks and fat guys from Sheffield kneeling down beside
you and chatting as if you belonged there. I was so proud
of you. I am so proud of you. I will never leave you,
Charlie. Never. I'm going to try to sleep now.

Bless you, darling.

Daddy

My darling,

It is Robbie's birthday. He is sixteen. It seems unbelievable. He didn't get very many presents but he didn't mind. Chitson bought him a really cool black and white guitar strap and Chitson's mum made a huge chocolate cake which is not really a cake, just a huge block of melted chocolate.

I have just arrived home. It's after 8 p.m. and I have had a terrible row with Oma. I don't quite know how it happened. I went to see her because I have been worried about her and what started out as a gentle conversation about the bridge club turned into a horrible argument. I tried not to argue but you know how patronising I sound when I talk quietly. I should have kept my mouth shut. I left Oma crying and I punched her best armchair so hard that I have bruised the bone in the side of my hand. But you came to me in the car and told me not to worry and said that Oma was Oma and things would be all right. I didn't consciously think about you, you were just there, so clear that I could almost touch you.

Oma loved you so much. She loves you so much. She cannot bear it. She looks as if she has been crying all the time, huge dark circles surround her eyes and her body shudders every few minutes as she fights to control the tears. I can't bear her grief but I can't live with her constant disapproval. I know now, after so many years, what gnaws away at her soul. She cannot abide to see lost potential, a good mind wasted.

I remember now what started the argument. I said I wouldn't mind if I had to be a dustman. I will do what I have to do to pay the bills. Oma does mind if I become a dustman. When you were here all I really cared about was that all of you would find happiness. You could have been a ballet dancer or a barmaid. I really wouldn't have minded so long as it made you happy. I can hear you as I type. 'It's none of your bloody business anyway.' That's what you would have said. And you would have been right. I rang Auntie Trish on my way home and asked her to ring Oma to check that she is OK. If you can hear me, will you go to her too? I'll be with Mummy tonight and Robbie and Cheese are here and, of course, Horsey who is very tired because he spent two hours cleaning the house. He really is amazing. You would hate him even more although I know you loved him really.

We are going to take a cake in for Robbie with sixteen candles. He'll never be able to blow them out now he has a twenty-a-day habit, well, five at least. I have tried to stop him but not really hard enough. He will smoke whether I want him to or not and what kind of example have I been? I am trying to be cheerful for Robbie. He knows you love him and you know that he loves you. Last night he told me that he wants to learn to sing and that he is going to start writing the words to songs as well as the music. I didn't ask him what he wanted to write about but he said that he had a lot of things he wanted to say and that Charlie [McPartland] only wanted to write songs called 'You're Scum' with no tune or emotion. I think Robbie wants to write about you.

I love you. Night–night, sleep tight. I'll come up and see you, I promise.

Your Daddy

Hello, my sweetheart,

Somehow, beyond our understanding, each day gets worse. Few people come now although Paul and Mel come when they can and John Keeling rings every day. Terry and Sylvie have been wonderful too and, of course, the irrepressible Mrs Wiggett who always takes time off from any suspicious activities to ring. Auntie Trish rings on most days as well although Uncle Davy is suffering. He misses Dan so much and he misses you. He worries incessantly about his businesses and I cannot help him at the moment. I can't leave Mummy, certainly not before six in the morning. I have to try to get Robbie and Horsey ready for school and drive them. Mummy cannot drive. The weight of her grief is slowly crushing her. We are going to see a counsellor on Friday in a place called Fulbourn near Cambridge. I will let you know how it goes. In the meantime we have some pills from the doctor. I told you, I think. Today we both took our third pill. Maybe they will begin to work soon.

We are going to move to Newport if we can. I spotted a small terraced house which is available to rent. We will have to sell this first so I am going to go out this afternoon and buy paint and rollers and start redecorating myself. God knows what the place will look like when I've finished. I know how badly you wanted to move to Newport and live next to Spuggy in the 'hood. This house isn't in the 'hood exactly but it is near by, just up Wicken Road behind the school, only a five-minute walk from Cheese's house. I think you will approve if we can get it. I would like a house with an open fire. It doesn't have to be a big house, in fact the smaller the better. Paul and Mel's council house is tiny but they have made it so cosy. I love their sitting room. It is so small that Terry and Sylvie couldn't fit even one of their sofas into it but I prefer it. Terry and Sylvie's living room is the length of a bowling alley and has the atmosphere of a Spanish holiday home and that's without the life-size wooden dogs lying unexpectedly behind doors like discarded Cluedo murder weapons. I was at Terry's the other day and mistook a slumbering wooden beagle for the real thing.

Darling one,

I didn't mean to finish so abruptly last time. Mrs Wiggett and John Keeling both came without warning and stayed until past eleven. By that time I was too worn out to write. I had taken a diazepam and sleep beckoned. I only just had the energy to put the beds up in the living room. Part of me thinks we should try to maintain some kind of routine but neither Mummy nor I can bear the thought of going upstairs. Only Robbie regularly uses his room. We hear him playing the guitar every night until the early hours. Cheese almost lives here now. I worry for her mother who must miss her but Cheese says they are getting on better now than ever before and her brother Will is at home. I must not let the situation get out of hand but she comforts Robbie in a way that we can't.

I went to the school yesterday to talk to the headmaster, Mr Priestley, about Robbie mainly but also about Horsey. Mr Priestley is a good man. He spoke beautifully at your service. The school will make a special consideration with regard to Robbie's GCSEs. All they ask is that he attends classes and does his best. Under the circumstances they understand that he is finding it almost impossible to concentrate. What lasting damage may have been done only time will tell.

Life, for most people, has returned to normal as it must. Neither Mummy nor I can escape from the horror. We received a phone call this morning from a lady called Sue whom we hardly know. She is the wife of the man who runs Go Express, the courier company. We received the most beautiful bouquet of flowers from them and a card signed by everyone at the company. Sue told me that she and her husband had lost their daughter. I didn't ask how old she had been but Sue told me that she would be twenty-one now, and only five years ago she lost her grandson as well. She said it does get worse and it probably will get worse still but eventually we will learn to cope. There is no short cut and, in a way, I am glad. I can't bear to live without you but I am frightened of not missing you. People say that you will always be a part of us and that the memories will grow more vivid with time. It is no consolation.

I have tried during these past weeks to keep a perspective. It is something I have always done and now I think, maybe, that this kind of forced reasonableness has made life more difficult. Every day thousands of children die and many of them have been loved as passionately as you have been. Their parents' grief cannot be any less than ours. We are part of a club that nobody wants to join and it is growing bigger every day. But there is no comfort to be gained from the suffering of others. We know why we must go on, for Robbie and Horsey and because it's what you would have wanted. So many people tell us that. Normally I just smile and nod my head but the other day I could not contain my anger and I told a lady, 'I'll tell you what Charlie would want, she would want to be here, that's what she would want. To have her whole life ahead of her just like your daughter.' The woman was shocked and backed away from me. I felt and still feel guilty. I know the woman meant well but sometimes it's very hard.

Yesterday evening, before John and Mrs Wiggett made their grand entrance, I rang Auntie Trish. I didn't know who else to ring. Mummy was asleep and Horsey was playing on his playstation. Robbie was in Newport. I felt absolutely desperate. I couldn't breathe and I didn't know what to do with myself. I wanted to punch the walls as hard as I could, just smash whatever was nearest to me, scream at the top of my voice. Trish told me to talk out loud to you and that you would come. I begin to understand what she means. I went to sit in the car and I asked you for help. I begged you to come to me, to help us. You didn't come but after a while, once I had calmed down a little, I heard your voice in my head. 'It's all right, Daddy,' you said. 'I love you, Daddy.' And I love you so much. Then I realised that I have this huge mountain of love to give you but you are not there and I don't know what to do with it. It is your love. I can't divide it up between Robbie and Horsey and Mummy. They have their own oceans of love. Your love is for you.

So I will continue to love you just the same. Talk to you, cuddle you, dream about you, go shopping with you.

Perhaps just because I cannot see you, it does not mean that you are not there.

I have had to stop for a bit. I cooked Horsey another disgusting meal, potato waffles, sausages and beans, which he ate with some enthusiasm. Last night I made him burgers, chips and beans. John was watching me cook. 'Mmm,' he said, if indeed you can say Mmm. 'It almost makes Little Chef seem appealing.' I shan't be cooking for John in the near future.

The doctor came. Mummy was lying on the settee and I sat on the floor in front of her, holding her hand. Her diet of one banana and a half-cup of soup a day is not going to make her strong. She has lost more than a stone in weight and she was hardly a Russian shot-putter to begin with. Doctor Tayler is more concerned that she is drinking sufficient fluids which I think she is. I still eat although I no longer care what. Sometimes I'll eat sausages and beans along with Horsey or if not a bowl of cereal and toast. Robbie stays in Newport most nights until at least ten o'clock. He eats at Cheese's house. I shall have to make some contribution to her mother's shopping bill.

It's Alan Wiggett's birthday today. Jill told us that he wanted anybody who was prepared to buy him a present to give money to the NSPCC for you instead. He really is a good man. I have grown to like him very much.

Tomorrow we are going to see the counsellor at ten in the morning. I will let you know how we get on. I just persuaded Mummy to eat a quarter of a Danish pastry.

I love you, darling. I think about you with every
waking moment. I don't dare dream so I have taken a
diazepam. One day, maybe, I will find the courage.
Sleep well.

Daddy

Hello, my darling,

It is about seven in the evening. Robbie has come back
from Newport with a whole gaggle of friends, Cheese,
Lou, Calvert and Charlie McP. They're up in his room at
the moment, no doubt smoking or something worse.

We went to see the psychiatrist today, a man called
Neil Hunt, small and very dapper with red hair and a
kind, thoughtful face. He asked Mummy to talk about her
feelings and Mummy said that all she can do is focus on
that day and relive the horror over and over again. It is
the same for me although I can sometimes push it away. It
is a physical thing. Dr Hunt felt that we had to try to
reintroduce some kind of routine, however mundane.
Sleeping upstairs instead of in the sitting room. Cooking
simple meals at prescribed times. I didn't like to tell him
that we have never done that. He was worried about
Mummy not eating and said that he would need to see
her again if her weight drops any further. As for the rest,
there is no short cut, no easy route. How can there be? It
is a life sentence but one that we may get used to in time.

Adele came round at midday. We had only been back a
few minutes. She brought a picnic basket full of home-
cooked food. Butternut squash soup with Thai chilli sauce,

which is delicious. Mummy has yet to try it but promises that she will. Home-made apricot jam and garlic bread. Not a bad haul considering I haven't been shopping for days.

She says that Bee has started to write to you in the form of a diary. She has been more like her old self ever since Mummy gave back her hair straightening machine. That was a weird experience. About a week ago we went to see Robbie Gladwell in his studio in Bulmer, but you probably know that already as Robbie claims you are with him virtually all the time. He said that you had a friend with whom you had fallen out and she needed something back, something that was still in your room. Mummy and I had no idea about the hair straightener but Robbie mentioned that it might be a set of curling tongs. I find these psychic phenomena very strange. Most of the people who come to see us have a story to tell. Apparently, a couple of weeks ago you locked Mel and Paul's bathroom door from the inside so that no one could go to the loo. According to them both it is impossible to lock the bathroom from the inside unless you are actually in the bathroom. I must admit it is the sort of thing that you would do. Not much later you unscrewed Mrs Wiggett's bathroom mirror and left it lying on a towel completely undamaged. What is it with you and bathrooms?

Do you remember Mummy's cousin Kate and her husband Roger? You met them at Gerard's (Mummy's cousin) wedding. About nine months ago Roger's son Justin killed himself. He was twenty-three. I have spoken to Roger on several occasions. Justin was his son from his

61

first marriage, before he met Kate. Roger had no idea that Justin was even depressed. They talked every day and saw each other several times a week. Roger adored him. At least I know you were happy. I do know that. I do not know how one could go on after such a thing happening. I do not know for sure that I can go on. I tell myself I have to for Robbie and Horsey and Mummy but with each new day the cold reality draws me further in and I am struggling.

I can hear Robbie and the others playing their guitars and singing. They are playing a Green Day song for you. I am crying. You would love it so much. You would be singing the loudest and screeching at them to 'shut up a minute' while you persuaded them to play a different song. They all miss you, talk about you constantly, hug each other between lessons or when they see each other in the street. You have united a school and brought the best out of everybody. I will not let this be the end. Somehow it must be a beginning.

I am going to try to sleep. Even though the psychiatrist said we had to sleep upstairs, we are not ready. We may have to tomorrow night as Horsey is having a party and five of his friends are staying.

I love you, darling. Night–night.

Daddy

My sweetheart,

I didn't write yesterday (Saturday). I'm sorry. It was Horsey's party and the house was too full of noise and chaos to find the time or the necessary peace to think, let alone write. I thought, maybe, having the place full of children would help but it meant that Mummy and I had to spend the whole night sitting in the kitchen, disturbed occasionally by bloodcurdling screams or by a succession of small boys demanding drinks or cakes or both.

We have taken down all the sympathy cards and put them in a pile in the sitting room next to the bookcase. Mummy had made them into a collage on the mirror in the kitchen. An ever growing gallery of pictures of you has risen to take their place. We sat mostly in silence in the dark, the only light cast from a candle that we bought from that lovely gift shop by the church. I held Mummy's hand and we drank tea and smoked endless cigarettes. There is not much to say. I cannot work because I cannot leave Mummy alone.

Robbie, too, is mostly silent. He must suffer terribly. His friends say he is brilliant at school, still making the others laugh and comforting them when they are in need. I fear for him but he knows we will do anything to help him. I have spoken to the school again about his GCSEs and he is under no pressure. All they want him to do is attend classes. Horsey alone seems almost unaffected. I can't risk making that assumption so I have asked his form teacher to keep an eye on him.

Once the partygoers had fallen asleep, Mummy and I slept on that green fold-out settee in the computer room and tried to watch a film on your television. I took it from your room. I hope you don't mind. I also accidentally switched off your CD player. I had an old copy of *Bridget Jones's Diary*. I think Mummy watched it all. I couldn't bear it. We slept fitfully and I awoke while it was still dark. I can't lie in bed any more, not that I ever could. There is no comfort. No escape from the monster. I am frightened that I am falling into depression. We are at the bottom of a well and I can no longer see the light, only the darkness and the closeness of the walls. Anyway I went to get the papers from the Spar and sat at the kitchen table with a cup of tea and a piece of toast and marmalade. The papers can be a distraction but I am becoming more and more sick of them. The Sunday papers are the worst, especially the so-called broadsheets with their appalling supplements full of stories about people for whom the word trivial is woefully inadequate. Maybe my rage at this rubbish is a sign of my depression or maybe I just shouldn't read it.

Your cousin Toby and his girlfriend, Laura, paid us a surprise visit at about half past two. They drove from London and stayed until past six. I felt guilty because we were lousy company. Toby played chess with Horsey and forced an honourable draw although Horsey cheated by whistling and snapping his fingers throughout. This kind of gamesmanship will have to stop or nobody is going to take him on any more. Toby brought a letter he had received from Tony Blair. I had had no idea that Toby had written in the first place. The Prime Minister's reply was very courteous but ultimately useless. The rail inquiry results won't be published for at least six months. I have already sent all the newspaper cuttings and various relevant internet stories to the lawyers. Soon I will find out whether we can sue Network Rail but even if the lawyers say we can't, I will not rest. We will build a bridge over the track, I promise you.

It is seven weeks now. Seven weeks without you. And then it will be seven months and then seven years. I cannot bear it. The doctor, the psychiatrist, the vicar, even our friends, some of whom understand because they too have suffered loss, say it will get easier to cope with in time. They say that we will get used to you not being here. I DON'T WANT TO GET USED TO YOU NOT BEING HERE.

I drove over to Sudbury this morning, leaving Mummy with Horsey and his friends. I went to Uncle Davy's factory to pick up some hamper materials. We had two orders on Friday. On the way I listened to the radio. It was a report from Serbia about identifying the bodies of innocent people killed during the Bosnian war who had been buried in unrecorded mass graves. Even now, ten years later many survivors cannot be sure of the fate of family members who disappeared during that terrible conflict. A woman was interviewed who had lost twenty-three close relatives including her husband and all of her children. How does she go on? We have lost you, and Uncle Davy has lost Dan, and I honestly do not know how we will survive.

I long for you with all my heart and soul and I will love you for ever.

Your Daddy

Good morning, my angel,

Horsey is at home again. He awoke with a terrible
headache and he is still sleeping now even though it is
11.15 a.m. Mummy is asleep too. I will not wake her. I
have written to the lawyers this morning, urging them to
make haste in preparing the case against Network Rail. I
can think of little else. I have also called the job centre,
enquiring as to whether we can claim any benefits. We
will get by, I'm just not sure how. The house is quiet, the
only sounds are the humming of the computer and a
vague rumbling noise from under the kitchen floor. I have
cleaned the kitchen and tried to read the paper but very
little grabs my attention.

I meant to tell you, I walked up to the Co-op on
Saturday to buy provisions for Horsey and his party guests.
The sun was shining and the sky was a clear winter blue.
We would have gone for a walk together in the afternoon,
across the fields behind the house or maybe up to the
windmill and down through the fields to the stream. I saw
you hiding on the steps up to the Guildhall. I saw you in
the red phone booth outside Gustav Holst's house. I saw
you walking in front of me, turning your head round to
check I was there, sucking your thumb as always.

Dear Charlie

Last winter we walked down to the stream after it had been raining for about a week. The stream had turned into a raging torrent and you wanted to go fishing even though I told you that all the fish would have been swept away. We bought a net and you spent several fruitless minutes dangling it from the bank, scooping up leaves and twigs and bits of old carrier bag. Eventually you decided that the only way to catch fish was to get into the river and track them down yourself. I tried to persuade you not to but I don't think I ever succeeded in persuading you not to do anything. It was freezing cold and probably dangerous although I was there and I felt sure that I could leap in and get you if you slipped or the current was too strong. You ignored me anyway and jumped straight in, the water almost up to your waist. You screamed because the water was so cold and then you started laughing and wading forwards at the same time, net held high. Horsey was with us, watching from the safety of the bank as I struggled along the edge by the water, just within grabbing range. Soon the water was up to your chest and I started to get worried but you scoffed at me and told me to 'get real'. The water must have been freezing. I kept nagging you to come out but you wouldn't, not until you reached the bend in the stream where you knew the fish were. You didn't catch a fish and remarkably, you didn't catch a cold either. When I pulled you out, you were giggling and shivering and shaking yourself like some shaggy old farm dog. I gave you my sweatshirt and you walked home soaking wet, squelching past the windmill, grumbling about the stupid fish.

I don't know how to live without you. Nothing seems real any more. I read on a bereavement site on the internet that people often think that the whole ghastly thing must be a dream until they eventually come to terms with their loss. I can't see how I will ever come to terms with a life without you. There will always be a space for you beside me whenever I walk. There will always be a seat beside me in the car that is just for you. There will always be a place in our bed for you to cuddle us in the morning.

I feel sick all the time now, a knotted feeling in the pit of my stomach. Mummy wears a hunted, desperate look. It is a struggle to get up in the morning and the smallest thing takes a tremendous effort. I don't really want to do anything any more, not even sleep. I just want not to be.

I love you. I will always love you wherever you are. You brought me more joy than I ever thought was possible. I thought that you would be with me until the end and that you would be there to say 'goodbye' to me. I cannot imagine how this has happened.

Bless you.

Daddy

Good morning, my angel,

I am sorry I didn't write yesterday. It was a very strange day. The sun shone from a wonderful washed-out blue sky and frost clung to every skeletal branch and blade of grass. I tried to focus on the beauty and not think of the past or the future and in that way find a moment's peace. I think today is the ninth day since we started taking the pills and maybe they are having some effect. I feel less desperate but when you are in my mind, which is all the time, where once you were clear and vivid, I see you now behind a veil of mist.

I am staring at a picture of you that Mummy pasted to the wall above the computer. It was taken last summer at Uncle Davy's house whilst we were sitting outside on their fancy new patio. You look thoughtful but not sad, looking away from the camera. In fact I do not think that you were aware that someone was taking your picture. It was before you had your hair cut and those extraordinary auburn curls are lying across your shoulders. I wonder what you are thinking. You are so beautiful and the knot in my stomach is twisting tighter and tighter.

The police came at around midday to take a statement for the inquest. Mummy slept on the settee. I knew she would not be able to bear having to talk about what happened. The policeman has been to see us before. His name is Peter and he has been trained in the art of gentle interrogation. He asked me to talk about you so that the court would be able to form a picture of what you were like. I said I could talk about you for a hundred years without stopping or once repeating myself. How could I present my daughter's life on two pages of handwritten paper?

Peter helped me by asking questions. He wanted to know your full name, Charlotte Grace Emily Thompson, and where you were born. You were always proud that you had been born in Bury St Edmunds and not in Harlow or Chelmsford like Horsey and Robbie. My Essex boys and my Suffolk girl. He wanted to know whether you had any hobbies. I told him that life was your hobby and that you had been happy and, when I thought about it, I could not think of a single time that you had been ill, really ill, I mean. You had never been in hospital or once been so ill that we had had to call out the doctor. I told him about your fantastic poems and that you had been chosen to represent the school in a creative writing competition. With each word, with each memory, I found myself becoming more hollow.

And then I had to describe the day itself, something that I have tried with all my might not to do, not to speak about it or think about it, although at night, alone in the creeping dark, the monster comes and I cannot look away. At last Peter seemed content with the information that I had given him and as a parting shot, he

gave me a bag of clothes that you had left at Livvy's
house. I had to sign a form to say that I had received
them, another signature on a piece of paper
acknowledging that you have gone.

That was yesterday. Another gate closed. Some other
things happened. I went to Sudbury once Horsey and
Robbie had returned home to keep Mummy company.
I needed to buy some films for some more hamper orders
and I wanted to see Oma. She is alone much of the time,
imprisoned with her memories just like us. Uncle Davy's
shop didn't have the films, obviously, but Oma had made
a shepherd's pie for me to take home. We sat and talked
for half an hour without arguing. She is mostly worried
about me now. She told Auntie Trish that she is
concerned for my safety and because we have no money
and soon we will have nowhere to live. That's what she
thinks anyway. I will find us somewhere to live as I always
have.

I drove home in the dark past Hedingham Castle and
on through Finchingfield near where we saw the ghost of
the old man. I imagined you resting your head in my lap
as you did when you were very tired and I stroked your
hair and traced the outline of your ear with my finger.
Somebody said that one day I will smile when I think of
you. Now I grit my teeth to stop myself from screaming.

Today we have slipped a few more feet into the depths
of hell. I cannot breathe and the sick feeling in my
stomach makes my throat ache. Mummy hardly speaks and
I have nothing to say. I tell Mummy I love her and she
smiles wanly at me and whispers that she loves me too.

I tell her that we have Horsey and Robbie to look after and she nods silently, looking into the distance.

Mrs Wiggett came at lunchtime but even she was subdued. Where once there had been laughter, now there are long periods of silence followed by short exchanges. After all what is there to say? Uncle Davy and Auntie Trish turned up unexpectedly. Trish spent an hour talking quietly with Mummy while Davy and I sat in the kitchen surrounded by pictures of you and talked about the business, sandwich bars mainly. He is going to introduce a Charlie Special at Reggiano's and he is going to rename Thompson's Fine Foods as Charlie's Larder. Murray is coming tomorrow with some artwork for us to approve.

I know that I have to find the strength inside myself in order to carry on and I know I have to be strong for the others. I promise I will be. I won't let you down.

Horsey wants to use the computer now so I will write later or tomorrow.

I love you so much. You are always with me.

Daddy

Hello, darling,

It is 10.30 in the morning. Robbie is at home again. He awoke with a splitting headache and asked whether I could take him to school at break. I can imagine how difficult everything must be for him. He hates going to school but he has such a good mind. I do not blame him. None of us have been lucky enough to have teachers who inspired us. Robbie loves his music but, without that, the school has failed him. It is not the same for Horsey. He is naturally competitive and takes pride in his work for its own sake. For Horsey a good teacher is a bonus. Somehow we must guide Robbie through his GCSEs so that he can go to the sixth form and there, perhaps, things will be different. He misses you and he feels that he is unimportant. He and Horsey are the most important people in the world. I am going to wake him up now and try to take him. Later I have to ring the lawyers and then Murray is coming.

Robbie didn't go to school after all. I wrote a letter to the head of year and hopefully she will understand how hard he is finding it. Cheese told me that last October, or around that time anyway, she and Robbie and some others had been asking each other what was the worst day they had ever had. Robbie told them that it was the day Dan died. I hadn't realised how profoundly Dan's death had affected him. And now this has happened to you.

Murray came at half past one wearing a very strange knee-length corduroy jacket. He was unshaven, with white sideburns and jet-black hair. He fascinates Mrs Wiggett who keeps inviting him to dinner along with John Keeling. As she says, John is the only handsome TV producer she has ever met. She told us she once knew an ugly TV producer but he didn't count.

Murray brought some logo ideas for Charlie's Larder. I quite like one of them but I find it almost impossible to talk or think about you in a way that acknowledges what has happened. I can talk about you but only in the present tense. You will have to let me know whether you like any of the ideas.

I think the pills may have started to work. I feel detached and you are still with me but the pain has been dulled. I don't know exactly what is going on. In a way I don't want the pain to be dulled. I don't want to feel 'normal'. I am terrified of not having you with me during every waking moment and I feel guilty if time passes when I realise that I have not thought of you and the enormity of the horror that has befallen us all is pushed, however briefly, to one side.

Mummy is cooking a roast dinner for Robbie and Horsey. It is the first time she has cooked anything other than potato waffles and sausages. Perhaps the pills are starting to work for her too. She ate some chunky Italian vegetable soup as well although I don't think she will be sharing the chicken.

I rang the lawyers this afternoon to see whether they think we have a legal claim. Network Rail have not even written to us. I am beginning to hate them, a deep hate growing inside me. I promise you, Charlie, I will never give up.

On the way back from picking up Horsey from school I called in to see Jim Lamb at Debden Green. Jim is another member of our terrible club. Thirty years ago his wife and fourteen-month-old son were killed in a car crash. Jim had been driving the car. It wasn't his fault but I don't think that provides much consolation. He married again, as you know, and James and Matt are his sons from his second marriage.

Jim invited me in and gave me a large shot of malt whisky. We stood in his kitchen, leaning against the work tops, surrounded by unpaid bills and yesterday's washing up. He asked after Mummy and when I told him how bad she is, I saw tears come to the corners of his eyes. He told me that after his wife and child died and he had finally been released from hospital, he went to see his local vicar. He asked the man why. He said he could understand God wanting to take a grown-up but what had a fourteen-month-old boy done to deserve what had happened? The vicar told him that he didn't have any answers but that this life is 'hell on earth' so there must be something better, a better place free from pain and suffering.

And this life is a 'hell on earth' for most people. Three thousand children a day die from malaria. Tens of thousands are swept away by tsunamis or buried in the aftermath of earthquakes. Half the world lives in abject poverty. In the West we kid ourselves that we are lucky with our money and our possessions but we have forfeited our spirituality. We want to live for ever because we dare not hope to live again. I want to find you, darling, to find the belief. The Buddhists believe that the spirit is reborn after forty-nine days and that all life goes through an eternal cycle of death and rebirth. Robbie told me last night that he would like to be a Buddhist. So would I.

I must stop now. Mummy is serving up the chicken and I will eat some. I will write later or tomorrow. I love you more than anything.

Your Daddy

27 January 2006

Hello, poppet,

It's late, about midnight on Friday. The Wiggetts came round and brought us a takeaway from the Indian. Robbie and Cheese are up in Robbie's bedroom listening to music. Mummy is watching a film in the sitting room and Horsey is asleep.

Somehow yesterday I felt detached but the full horror has returned today. I had to go to London for Uncle Davy this morning, to St Hubert's Foods in Tottenham to pick up several cases of full-fat Greek cheese. I have no idea what he does with it. We went there together on several occasions. It was my first time without you. I tried to be strong but I broke down and parked in Tesco's car park and cried and howled your name. There are times when I am distracted but they are brief like punctuation marks in an endless sentence. The misery is relentless because I cannot escape from my own mind, which replays what must have happened to you on an infinite loop. I see you laughing, holding hands with Livvy, full of life and hope, and then, suddenly, you are gone, wiped out. I cannot even remember the last words I said to you or what we did on the Friday night.

All the time, day by day, the anger grows inside me.

This shouldn't have happened. It wasn't a tragic accident. It wasn't just a case of being in the wrong place at the wrong time. It wasn't an act of God. It was something that shouldn't have been allowed to happen. I'm sorry, darling. I'm too upset and too angry to write. I think it's better if I write again in the morning when I am calmer. There are lots of happier things to tell you about.

I love you.

Daddy

28 January 2006

Hello, my angel,

I am sorry but it is not the morning. It is late afternoon and today has been no different from yesterday. Mel C came to see us this morning but Mummy was sleeping so we sat in the kitchen and smoked about ten cigarettes each and drank tea. She was really lovely. She said that she felt blessed that she had known you for five wonderful years and that she would do anything to help us, cut off her right arm to bring you back for a day. She kept telling me how strong I'm being but I don't feel strong. I feel sick all the time and the emptiness inside me is growing. Reverend Titford e-mailed us again. He says he thinks of us every day, especially in the mornings, and that he knows that you are in a better place.

Do you remember Bernard, my financial adviser? You met him once when he came to Debden Green. He rang several days ago because he had been away over Christmas and did not know what had happened. He actually helped me and I am trying to cling on to what he said like a drowning man clinging to a branch. He said that he KNEW you were OK. 'It's a FACT,' he said. I asked how he knew and he said he just did. He was so certain and I was comforted by his certainty. I wish Mummy had been able to speak to him. I remembered that he had been very ill about four years ago. He had a very serious heart attack and, at one point, in the hospital, he was declared dead but he came back. He told me that he saw the light. It is a story that I have read about many times but Bernard is the only person I know who has first-hand experience. I want him to be right.

I have been studying Buddhist chants and I am thinking of trying to take Mummy and Robbie and Horsey to Tibet, to the holy city of Lhasa, which is the highest city in the world. The chant goes like this: OM MANI PADME HUM. It is the holiest chant in the Buddhist religion and if you have faith and understanding this chant will protect the spirit and guarantee a happy rebirth. I cannot pretend that I have faith and understanding but I want to try to find faith and, through faith, gain understanding. If we go to Tibet, to the heart of Buddhism, we may begin to understand. I cannot believe in the Christian God although I am not certain enough to turn my back completely. A good and wise man like the Reverend Titford would not devote himself to the Christian Church without belief. We try to draw strength from all of these sources but nothing can compensate for your loss.

I must go now to pick up Robbie. He is having a band practice and we are going to drive over to see John Keeling for a couple of hours. I will try to write more later.

I love you so much.

Daddy

My sweetheart,

It is Sunday morning. The sun is shining and I have
been staring out through the kitchen window across the
fields where we used to walk. Mummy has been reading
the paper and Horsey is watching television. Robbie is in
his bedroom with Cheese playing the guitar. The house is
quiet. Mummy and I barely talk because we do not know
what to say to each other. The affection between us
remains and we hold each other's hands in silence.
Somehow we put on a brave face for Robbie and Horsey
or when friends come but it requires an enormous effort.
Even the smallest task seems beyond us. In truth I don't
want to do anything. The utility room needs to be
cleaned and the house is getting dustier and dustier. I
manage to wash up and cook rudimentary meals. Mummy
has had moments when something has spurred her into
action but mostly all she can do is sleep. I know that we
must try to do as much as possible, that the more we do,
the more distractions we create for ourselves, will only
help us to go on, but I have no work. Without money I
cannot generate any hamper orders and I have no money.
I would do anything but Mummy cannot be left alone.
We cannot pay the bills and I will have to ring the

mortgage company and ask them to put our payments on hold.

Oma is beside herself with worry and, like us, she is drowning in grief. She has lost two grandchildren in less than a year and beyond that it is now thirty-three years since my father died. That is a long time to spend alone. When I think of what our family has suffered over the past years, it is easy to think that we may be cursed. I push this thought away because no good can come of it and it is dangerously self-pitying but however hard I push, the thought always returns like an itch, at first barely noticeable and then growing in intensity. And with this terrible thought comes fear. If anything were to happen to Robbie or Horsey, then our lives would certainly be over. The fear, the longing and the misery are physical weights that pin us down, making each step, each action, sometimes each thought an almost impossible burden.

When I write to you, I feel closer to you even though I am sure you do not want to hear most of what I have to say. This writing provides an outlet for me, not only a way to remember but a means to heal the wound. We may not be physically injured but our injuries are terrible nonetheless and just like a person with appalling physical injuries, we must learn to do the basic things again. And sometimes we lose the will to go on. There are times when I do not think about you although part of my mind knows I am not thinking about you and tells me, so that in effect I am thinking of you, just not in a specific way. I think this happens when the mind simply becomes overloaded with grief and shuts down. I find myself

watching television like a zombie or idly smoking a
cigarette, staring at the wall.

You know I told you I was going to start painting the
house and preparing it for sale? I think that was more than
a week ago. I haven't started yet. I keep thinking about it.
Maybe I will start this afternoon. I will let you know.

The pills with the unpronounceable name that the
doctor gave us seemed to work for a few days although it
is hard to remember now. I think I struggled to visualise
you but now you are back, in every chair, lying on the
sofa with your legs dangling over the arm, kicking your
feet and sucking your thumb, standing in the doorway to
the sitting room wrapped in your duvet, opening and
closing the fridge as if each time something would appear
that hadn't been there before, sitting on the kitchen work
surface and leaping on to my back when I turned away
from you. Do you remember how you used to run at me
when we were outside and you had enough room to
build up some serious momentum during the run-up? I
would stand sideways on, feet braced for impact, shoulder
leaning slightly forward, and you would buffalo into me at
speed, trying to knock me down. At the very least you
would send me reeling and stumbling twenty feet
backwards. Who will try to knock me down now?

It's nearly three in the afternoon. We would probably
have walked up to the Spar at least twice by now, once
the back way up past the bowling green and down
through the avenue of elderberry bushes that leads out on
to the main road. I liked that way. It was always more
interesting than walking along the road past the chip shop.

I cannot walk there any more, not without you. I drive to the Spar now. Every paving stone holds a memory of you, every garden wall that you would sit on to wait for me as I struggled home laden down with shopping bags although you would carry them the last hundred yards to demonstrate your strength and to show Mummy how lazy your father was. And by now you might even be doing some homework or watching television or sitting in your room listening to music or, more likely, on MSN arranging secret assignations with boys.

We went to see John Keeling last night for a couple of hours. I think I told you. Mummy likes going to see John because he is direct and thoughtful and he has his own crosses to bear. He is also remarkably well read. We sat around his kitchen table in his small but neat new house while his two daughters, Amber and Seren, played with Horsey in the living room. Amber and Seren are ten and eight. You would love them. John spoke mainly to Mummy for which I was grateful because she, above all, needs the greatest attention and comfort.

John is fascinated by the stars as am I but he has the background knowledge to support his wonder. He told us that the stars are made out of magnesium and iron and that magnesium and iron courses through our bodies, that we are made of the same stuff as the stars themselves and that, in the words of Carl Sagan, we are 'children of the stars'. Charlie, John says you are out there now, experiencing wonders beyond our comprehension, freed from the constraints of time and physicality. He speaks with such passion and his eyes glow with the fervour of a fanatic. It is a wonderful idea and it is one that I can believe far more readily than the traditional concept of 'heaven'. But you are still not with us and your loss is an amputation and the wound is raw and bleeding. I think we will probably learn to live again but we may only ever be able to hobble, crippled by your loss, always remembering what it was once like to be whole.

I am going to take Horsey to play with a friend now. I miss you.

Your Daddy

I went to Newport to get Horsey's friend Billy. He is really nice but he reminds me of a small creature who lives in a river bank, a vole possibly or a water rat. He is frightened of everything. In the fading light on the way home he said that he thought that the hedgerows looked like clumps of ghostly broccoli, which he didn't like because he is frightened of broccoli. He is not frightened of cauliflower, you will be pleased to hear. They are both watching a film in the sitting room. Mrs Wiggett is here but Mummy is not really able to talk much any more so I think she will be going soon. I am too tired to engage in conversation.

The mind is an extraordinary thing. It must work on so many different levels at once. A part of my mind knows that you are gone but another part still refuses to accept it. As a result I live in a dream with occasional flashes of reality. When these flashes come they hit me with an almost physical force. I have to hold on to something to stop myself from collapsing. Sometimes, when I feel brave enough, I talk about how I feel to someone else.

Of all the terrible things that one imagines might happen during a lifetime, the death of a child can never be considered. I have imagined being diagnosed with a terminal illness. I have wondered how I would cope with divorce or the death of my mother or even Uncle Davy. I have experienced losing my job, my house and my income, and all these things are manageable with support and optimism. But this. Nothing prepares you for this and therefore the mind cannot accept it. If you lose your job, you can try to find another. If your mother dies, then maybe she has had a good life and she has lived to a reasonable age. But parents lose children every day. Two months ago I might have been watching the news, a terrible story about a murder or an accident, and I would have felt a moment's sadness or a detached feeling of compassion for the victims, but it would be fleeting and then our life would go on.

I wonder how other people cope but I am not drawn to talk to them. I have e-mailed Livvy's mother on several occasions and I have received a heartfelt reply each time but we have not met and shared our grief. I have only met Livvy's father once, at the service in Newport. I do not even have his telephone number. I think, for us, grief is a lonely thing. I hear that Livvy's mother and her sister, Stevie, have gone to Singapore for three weeks. I would like to go away somewhere and maybe not come back.

There are memories of you everywhere. Driving to school we pass that strange tree, our wishing tree, which

looks like a Mexican hatstand but turned out to be a
mobile phone mast disguised with fake branches. You and
I were the only ones who were taken in. Jim told us it
was a mobile phone mast, not quite sure whether we were
pulling his leg when we asked what kind of tree it was.
He told us that if you look closely you can see the
transformer and it doesn't look anything like a real tree
anyway. We walked up to it one day just to check and,
sure enough, Jim was right. Nothing changed for us
though. We still made our wish every day as we passed,
you hooking your little finger around mine. I don't know
what you wished for but I always wished for the same
thing. Nobody heard my wish.

I am so tired, Charlikins. Auntie Franky had an amazing
dream. I will tell you about it tomorrow.

Sleep well, my angel, I love you.

Daddy

Hello, my darling,

I think I begin to understand what is happening. With each passing day you are getting further away and as you get further away the true realisation that you won't be coming back gains in strength. I do not think that my memories of you will fade. In fact, as I get older I am sure that I will remember more and more and that I will be able to replay adventures and moments from each part of your life. Perhaps I will be able to catalogue every conversation, every journey, every new experience we shared and reference them like a library. And maybe this will bring comfort. But now, to watch you disappear over the horizon is more than I can bear.

Andy Nimmo came this morning and tomorrow he is going to start repainting the house so that we can sell it. I am going to help him. He has offered his services for nothing but I will pay him out of the proceeds of the sale. With his help the job should be done in a week. Later today Mummy and I will have to find the energy to start clearing the kitchen so that it is ready for its overhaul.

It has been a busy morning. Jim Lamb came to MOT the car and I have written some letters thanking people for the beautiful flowers they sent for you. One woman, a dinner lady at Mummy's school, brought the most extraordinary African plant in a purple vase with multicoloured beads for bedding. At first I thought it was a toy or at least made of plastic but it turned out to be real. The head of the plant or flower looked like a medieval arrow with vicious serrated edges. I was frightened that if I turned my back on it, it would attack me. Unfortunately we forgot to water it and it died.

Mummy is sleeping again. I have been looking up post-traumatic stress disorder on the internet and Mummy has all the symptoms. I have most of them myself. Recurrent nightmares, a tendency to sleep during the day, not eating, no desire to go out: the list goes on. I will have to go back to the doctor. I think we may need some more help.

Hello, poppet,

It's about 7 p.m. Mel Bowe rang and asked whether Mummy would help her to type up four essays that she has had to write for her advocacy qualification. Mel can't type because she is nearly blind. She has no peripheral vision and she can't distinguish between shapes if they are more than a few feet away. Mummy didn't want to go but Mel and Paul have been so supportive that she felt she couldn't let Mel down. I have just dropped her off and now Horsey and I are on our own as Robbie is in Newport with Cheese. I can hear Horsey playing '99 Red Balloons' on Robbie's guitar.

I find writing very difficult at the moment. I want to write because by sitting here and trying to communicate with you in a normal kind of way, I feel a connection, I even feel hope. If I can just keep writing I won't have to let you go. I remember about two months after Dan died, Uncle Davy phoned me to tell me that Dan had gone to Australia and that he was surfing on Bondi Beach. He's not dead, of course he isn't dead, he just went away. It doesn't matter how many times I read the paper or watch the news, trying to relate to other parents who have lost children and who appear to find a way to go on. Telling myself that I still have two wonderful children and a beautiful wife. That in the great scheme of things I must still count myself lucky. All I can think of is you. All I can think of is how, every day of my life, I prayed for your safety. I did everything I could to avoid angering the gods. For thirteen years I tried to protect you and yet, lurking in the back of my mind, behind a door that I cannot even find, let alone open, is a dark thought. One that may always have been there. Like a glimpse into another life I am only able to sense it but maybe I knew something would happen right from the very beginning.

I used to dream that I was forty-eight years old when I was in my twenties. Forty-eight seemed so old but why forty-eight? I am forty-eight now. The dreams were full of dread. Now that the dream has come back to me after all these years, I cannot shake off the notion that it must have been a premonition. Why forty-eight? It makes no sense. Perhaps my life is meant to end too. I appointed myself your bodyguard when you were born and I have failed you. My life is forfeit. I tried to anticipate every situation. I remember now the last words I said to you on Saturday morning. 'Be careful when you cross the road in Cambridge. It can hurt being run down by a bicycle.' Can there be irony in the midst of such horror?

I didn't want to write about such things. I wanted, when I started to write to you, just to talk about happy memories, to create words to go with the pictures in my head. To be able to look back and live with you again.

Forgive me, my angel. I love you so much.

Daddy

Hello, my darling,

A whole day has gone by. It is the evening of the last day of the month. Andy and I have been painting since early morning and the hall and the kitchen are now bright and fresh and probably saleable. Mel C has been here for the last couple of hours, distracting Mummy with stories about Harry Chapman's adventures in Australia at Christmas. She is also full of the most salacious gossip. Apparently one of Harry's friends has been seduced by the mother of another one of his friends. Mel is incensed and she is trying to persuade Andy to attack the woman with one of his extendable painting devices. Mel left about half an hour ago and I can hear Mummy cooking in the kitchen. She is singing softly to herself, a song of infinite sadness.

There is so little to say to each other. We are not ready to talk about you together which would be to admit to ourselves the truth. I have received forms from the Department of Social Security so that we can claim some money while neither Mummy nor I can work. I have been trying to fill in the forms, which are so long that each one requires a tree to itself just to provide the paper. There is a section in each that asks for details of our

children. I have not been able to fill it in. How can I not
put your details down? How can I pretend that you have
never existed? How can I put down what has happened to
you? You are and always will be my daughter. You are
with me now. I can hear your voice, feel the pressure of
your hand in mine. It is too much to bear. I can smell
you and feel your hair brushing up against my cheek.
How can you not be? I cannot fill in the form. Somebody
will have to do it for me and I will sign it. Nothing can
take away what has been, the thirteen glorious years we
had together.

Every day I must make the journey to the school and
back, passing the park in Debden where we would cycle
in the summer. I saw the swings this morning and that
strange thing like a breeches-buoy or maybe a ski lift,
which you used to love. We would both get on it at
once, somehow finding room on that plastic hub-cap-style
seat and, with our combined weight stretching the cable
to breaking point, we would set off from the platform and
hurtle the hundred yards or so to the end of the line,
bumping into the ground and whizzing round and round,
laughing hysterically. Sometimes Horsey would come with
us and he would stand in our way to provide you with a
target or to slow us down, which used to irritate you so
much. That was only last summer, less than six months
ago.

At night, when Robbie and Horsey are asleep, I stare at
their beautiful faces and find myself in the grip of the most
terrible fear. Horsey seems unchanged, his face squashed
into the pillow but at a slight angle, allowing him to

breathe, his amazing rubber lips pushed alarmingly in the direction of his right ear so that I expect to find his mouth on the side of his face in the morning. Robbie has always worn an air of melancholy in his sleep. He is so white and his face is long and angular like that of a medieval knight. He sleeps on his back with his head inclined slightly to the side. He rarely moves. It seems to me that I have spent my whole life checking you as you slept, stroking your hair away from your face, marvelling at your beauty, at nature's exquisite brilliance. Do you remember how I used to measure your noses with my thumb and index finger? Robbie always had the biggest nose although hardly comparable to my own colossal hooter. Your nose was perfect, is perfect. That is a philosophical question. Is your nose an IS or a WAS? To some who do not carry you with them all the time and for whom you will always be frozen in the past, your nose is probably a WAS. For me it can only ever be an IS.

On Friday nine weeks will have passed. A friend of mine told me today that we are in the eye of the hurricane. That now is the worst time because we are beginning to realise the truth. How can there ever be a better time? How can it be possible that we will ever be happy again or truly laugh or look forward to anything? I do not want to be happy or accept that you have gone. Oma says we have a duty to live for ourselves, not just to look after Horsey and Robbie. I lie awake at night staring into the dark, wondering how this has happened to us. I am in a grey hell where I cannot see the future and I am unable to properly look into the past. Images of you flow constantly through my mind but they are all from the last year. I have to think about earlier times, conjure up pictures of you, but all too often I am left in a state of numb, blank misery. A cold, acid weight lies in the pit of my stomach.

Mummy found another poem that you had written after we had argued. I remember reading it the first time and the guilt I felt and my absolute love for you. I promise you nothing has changed. I will love you absolutely for ever. And if some people say that when we die, that is the end, we return to the nothingness from which we came, then that is fine, but I do not think that. Here is your poem.

The Sun shines boldly upon the golden sheaves
The babbling brook gurgles in the silence of the
    springtime wood
The blossom smells so sweet upon the trees
The blue bird sings to the lark on the chimney
The cowslips in the meadow stand tall among the
    grazing cows
As we sit in the countryside
Just you and me

Never was a day so perfect
The bluebells and the foxgloves standing proudly by the
    stream
Never was a day so perfect
Just you and me

The snow sits softly upon the frosty grass
The bare trees and dappling light shadow gracefully
    across the horizon
The smoke from warm fires rises into the air
The robins sit upon a white brick chimney
The silhouettes of white horses stand lazily in fields
    nearby
As we sit in the countryside
Just you and me

Never was a day so perfect
The frosty flowers and frozen ponds sleep peacefully by
    day with glee
Never was a day so perfect
Just you and me

What a wonderful and beautiful world we live in
Even though some times may seem bad
As long as we share as much love and compassion
Everything will always be OK no matter what
Because the truth is
Everyone wants to share beauty with somebody else
Nobody wants to be alone
I am sorry
I love you.

No, Charlie, I am sorry and I love you. I used to pray,
just a little, not necessarily at night, just whenever I
thought of it. I haven't really prayed lately. I am going to
try to start and I will pray for you always.

Dear Charlie

I love you more than I can possibly say. I miss you more than I can bear.

Your Daddy

My darling,

It is Friday. I haven't written for a couple of days although I have been thinking only of you. Andy has been painting the house and I have been trying to help him. I didn't realise what a lousy painter I am. While Andy has painted the entire hall, the stairs and the upstairs landing, I have managed ten cupboards in the kitchen. Everything is brilliant white now and much brighter. I think you would like it. We are going to lay a new floor in the kitchen using the fake wooden planks Mummy bought nearly a year ago at Homebase. When it is all done we will put the house up for sale and with luck our move to Newport will happen sooner rather than later.

On Wednesday I went with Robbie to the school for the sixth form open evening. I had thought that he would not want to go but he seemed quite enthusiastic. Fortunately we were spared the rousing induction speech because Robbie told me it started at 8 p.m. when it had actually started at 7 p.m. He has chosen to do media studies, computing and music technology, which strikes me as very sensible. The music course will teach him how to record and mix different instruments, which is exactly what he wants to do. Media studies is something I can help him with, in theory anyway. I spoke to the earnest young head of department and told her about my other life when I used to have a proper job, working for Warner and FilmFour. She pretended to be quite impressed and asked whether I might find the time to give some lectures to the students next year. I said I would consult my diary! Computing is something everybody who ever wants to get a job should have up their sleeve.

On our way out I bumped into Mr Priestley who was very warm and concerned. He said that time would help us to come to terms with what has happened to you. I wonder how people know. Time will only teach us to live without you. It will never heal the pain.

It is Oma's birthday today. She is eighty-three. I went to Sudbury this morning to see her and left Mummy at home alone. It is the first time that I have had to leave Mummy without company. I was not happy but she said that she would be OK and I couldn't disappoint Oma. I didn't buy her a card or a present. I knew she would not accept a present as we have no money and even a token would have enraged her but she seemed upset that I hadn't brought a card. I couldn't do it. How can she have a happy birthday? I had no idea what to write in a card. I stayed with her for nearly three hours instead. We went to lunch at the Mill Hotel where Mummy and I were married and you and I would walk across the meadows at the back. We sat at a window so that I had no choice but to stare out at the fields and all I could see was you, gallumphing through the grass, chasing the ducks, hands pushed deep into the pockets of your jeans. Sometimes when we had had an argument you would walk in front of me, your shoulders hunched, your hands in your pockets, and I would call after you, saying that I was sorry, and you would ignore me or say 'Whatever' in that way that made me feel small and stupid. Then you would look over your shoulder at me, giving me a blank stare, forcing me to run up to you and beg for forgiveness. And afterwards you would say sorry to me even if it wasn't your fault which it mostly wasn't, and we would walk along side by side, occasionally bumping into each other, you always being much rougher than was strictly necessary, provoking me until I bashed into you using the full force of my extra poundage and knocked you flying.

I tried to listen to Oma while I watched you in the field. We ate steak and Guinness pie with fresh vegetables, which was very nice but Oma pronounced hers 'tough' so I ended up having two portions. Oma wants me to be a teacher. Even though I am forty-eight years old it is not too late but I am not sure whether I have the passion. I only want to write. Oma says being a teacher is a terrific job if you want to be a writer and I am sure she is right . . . only. Only I cannot think or apply myself. I can only think of you.

I will write more soon. I love you.

Daddy

My angel,

It is Sunday evening. Yesterday we were lucky. John
Keeling, Paul and Mel, and Jill Wiggett all came to see us.
I had intended to write but it would have been rude to sit
here at the computer with our guests standing in the
kitchen. Paul and Mel brought three bottles of wine and I
think we drank them all.

Eventually John and I stayed up until two in the
morning talking. His divorce has come through and he is
deeply upset. I believe that he still he loves his (ex) wife
but she now has someone else and this week she has gone
with her friend and John's two daughters to Bulgaria on a
skiing holiday. John returns home from work every night
to sit in an empty house and he is often lonely but he
admits that he would still not swap with us. He, at least,
has two living daughters and even though he does not see
them as much he would wish, he can dream about their
futures and look forward to an old age with Amber and
Seren to bring him comfort and warmth.

Inevitably we all drank too much and Mummy went to
bed at half past twelve. She says that only red wine allows
her to sleep but she did not eat anything and she looked
as ill as I have ever seen her. We both have hangovers

today, dull, throbbing headaches to complement our misery.

Robbie has been at home all day but we have hardly seen him. He came out of his room for some breakfast. He had been crying and I hugged him but it is hard to comfort him and he will only talk when he is ready. I am so proud of him. He has been to school and done his best in lessons where concentration must be nearly impossible. Horsey remains the strongest of us all. He goes to school, does his homework, rarely complains and continues to tell terrible jokes. Last night John taught him to play several songs on Robbie's guitar. He picks things up at remarkable speed. John says that if he practises he could end up being better than Robbie. Maybe they will end up in a band together. That would be something.

I wanted to walk up to the church today and light a candle for you but Mummy has not felt up to it and I don't want to go on my own. I try to talk to Mummy. I tell her that I know you are 'out there'. John believes this from a scientist's perspective, as a romantic scientist. To be able to go on, to be able to consider the future in any kind of positive way, I have to believe that the essence of you still exists. I know that I have whatever is left of my life to find you and I will never stop looking.

I watched the football this afternoon. You won't be very interested to hear that Chelsea won again. Andy and Mel Nimmo invited me to their house to watch the match but the last time I went there was with you and I am unable to face sitting in their living room without you to cuddle me and annoy Andy by talking through all the good bits. Tomorrow Mummy and I are going to see Doctor Tayler. I will let you know what he has to say.

I had a dream a few nights ago where I was travelling through space at a tremendous speed. I wasn't in a spaceship or even a spacesuit. I was just as I am. The stars were going by so fast that I could see them only as an almost continuous blur of light and then, after a while, I don't know how long, I was surrounded by pinpricks of light, so close that I could touch them. I cannot remember any more but I like to think that the tiny points of light were somehow you. I'm sure the dream came after a conversation with John about stars but the sensation of speed was like nothing I have ever experienced.

I will write more soon. I know that you will always be with me and nothing can take away all that we had.

I love you.

Your Daddy

Darling Charlikins,

It is the evening again. Mummy is quietly reading the paper in the kitchen and Horsey is playing a video game. Robbie is in Newport. I am going to get him later.

I ended up going to the doctor on my own. Mummy was asleep and I did not want to wake her. The doctor has prescribed some more pills. He asked me whether I thought they were working. I said that I had no idea. It is hard to imagine feeling worse and yet I am able to function. On that basis maybe they are working. He is coming tomorrow to see Mummy at home. I am becoming increasingly worried about her. She eats so little and has no energy and no wish to do anything. She rouses herself to wash shirts for Robbie and Horsey and she cooks for them more often than I do now but that is all she does. I had hoped to persuade her to help me paint but she is not up to it.

I drove to Sudbury at lunchtime to take back some films to Uncle Davy's shop and return an incredibly expensive bag of almonds which I tried to sell to the White Hart at Broxted but they weren't interested. My days as an almond salesman are numbered.

I went to see Oma, who was eating an omelette filled with mushrooms and bacon, both of which had seen better days. She had found a picture of you taken when we were on holiday in Spain. It was obviously very windy because your hair is out of control, wrapped around your face like a nest of dazzling copper-coloured snakes. You are peering at me through a small gap with one solemn eye. I must have done something to upset you although I cannot remember what. I examined the picture with quiet longing. I still cannot accept that you are gone. I will always be waiting for you to come home. Then Oma found another picture of you taken when you were about three. You are grinning, baring those scary baby teeth, your hair only a whisper of what was to come.

Auntie Trish believes in fate, that we all have a predetermined time. This knowledge brings her comfort but I find it very difficult to cope with and I find no solace in the idea. Looking at you, at all the pictures of you, it is impossible to imagine a time without you but it is equally impossible to bear the idea that you were destined to live for only thirteen years and to be taken from us in such a way. Auntie Franky says that we must let you go and that we will only be able to carry on with our lives once we have accepted that you have gone. I still cannot put down in words what happened to you. I cannot talk about it. I don't know that I will ever be able to talk about it. But I am powerless to control my own thoughts and I cannot escape the horror.

★　　★　　★

I have just returned from Newport with Robbie. He has asked me to take him to see a band in Cambridge tomorrow night. Cheese is ill and he has been tending to her. He was telling me the details as we drove home but all I could think about was our last trip to the Brixton Academy to see the Alkaline Trio in November.

You sat in the back with Livvy and Will Holt and Chitson. We were driving down the Mile End Road because we had just stopped at McDonald's to stock up on burgers and Coke and you were holding court as usual. I must have said something that you disagreed with because the next thing I knew, you had poured the entire contents of your super-sized Coke bucket over my head, complete with crushed ice. I was, to put it mildly, slightly shocked. A stunned silence followed. I think you actually succeeded in shocking yourself. Chitson may have said, 'Oh shit!' I think you were all expecting a traditional parental reaction. For some reason I was in a very good mood. I can't say that I enjoyed the stickiness. My hair was sticky. My hands were sticky. Even the steering wheel was sticky. I said nothing for several seconds. I considered how angry I should be and eventually I said in a quiet voice, 'You really shouldn't have done that, Charlie.' Then I ruined it all by laughing. You used to call me 'the best daddy in the world'. I'm not and I wasn't but I had my moments. Tomorrow night I will sit in the Portland Arms while Robbie and his mates are watching the band and I will think of you.

Bless you, my sweetheart.

Daddy

My darling,

I couldn't write yesterday. I thought that I had reached the point where I could no longer go on. As if I had been holding the world on my shoulders and suddenly the weight had become too much to bear.

Robbie hasn't been to school this week. On Monday he stayed at home for the doctor and the next morning I had asked him to have a shower. You know his aversion to washing. I must have raised my voice because he turned on me, accusing me of not caring how he felt. Mummy joined in, telling me that I was handling the situation in completely the wrong way. I just snapped. All I had wanted was for Robbie to have a shower. One shower a week doesn't seem unreasonable. It was as if a dam burst. All my defences just crumbled. I was a house of paper being washed away in the torrent. The tears wouldn't stop. I locked myself in the study so Horsey wouldn't see me. I cried for most of the day, the terrible longing for you consuming me. Mummy slept.

In the evening I pulled myself together enough to take Robbie, Cheese and Charlie McP to see Captain Everything at the Portland Arms in Cambridge. They now have an Eighteens and Over Only policy so I had to talk

our way in and then stay with them for the whole time. I
had a headache that would have downed a rhinoceros so I
sat in a corner in the bar and thought of you.

There are many people in situations like ours and most
of them do go on, maintaining their dignity and finding
ways to a kind of fulfilment. I know now that we have to
move and that we have to discard the skin of our old life
completely. I ask myself whether this is running away but
I don't want the memories that are tied to this house. We
didn't want to move here in the first place. We never
wanted to leave Debden Green. This house was always
going to be a way station to another destination. And now
it will be forever haunted by your absence. It will be ten
weeks on Saturday and still we have not shut your door
or moved anything in your room. I do not know what
we will do when we come to move. Maybe Auntie Trish
will come and pack your room for us. I don't know how
I will feel in a different house, making a new start without
you. I know that I won't be without you, that you will
be in my every thought but for now that is no
consolation.

Sweetheart, I have to go now.

I will write again soon.

Bless you.

                    — Daddy

Hello, poppet,

It is Friday again. I couldn't write yesterday. It was a very bad day. Every day is a very bad day.

Oma asked me how I was and I said the same. What does she expect? How can we change from one solitary day to another? I tried to explain. Nothing will be any different tomorrow. We will wake up and you won't be there. There will be a second when we first open our eyes, while the edges of our dreams are still seeping away, when there is hope, when you might still be asleep in your bed, but you are not and our bodies know you are not even if our minds seek to trick us. So how can tomorrow be different?

I had the worst of dreams the other night. I dreamt that it was all a dream. Life is cruel whether you are awake or asleep. I know now what the future holds. Eventually we will wear a suit of armour that tells the outside world that we are OK. We will talk and laugh with others and keep our misery to ourselves. Meanwhile the layers of protective shock are being stripped away and soon we will be naked in the face of the truth.

Our friends are amazing. Paul and Mel Bowe and Mrs Wiggett came again last night but there is less and less to say. Mrs Wiggett spent the whole evening sending text messages to a secret admirer while Alan was having dinner at the Savoy. Mel brought some forms from the housing association because we may have a chance to get a council house.

Paul drank two gallons of beer and did some hilarious impressions of an old woman stuck in a barrel. He may have been doing an impression of something else but he wasn't specific. He has decided to go on a diet next week. We were all party to the pledge. He is going to eat only broccoli and brown rice and he will drink only red wine and no beer. Mel and Miles are going to move in with us. As vegetarians they are aware of the perils that lie ahead.

I spoke to the lawyers this morning. They have had nearly two weeks to consider the evidence. As time goes by I feel a cold fury building inside me. I cannot talk to Mummy about it because she cannot bear it. I cannot bear it either but I have to do something. I was trying to explain to Auntie Trish. Our grief may be no greater or no less than that of other parents who have lost a child but we are cursed by the belief that what happened to you and Livvy should not have been possible. It wasn't an act of God or a car accident or even a disease, all things no less ghastly but all at least explicable. I want revenge, pure and simple. I know that if I find it I won't feel any better afterwards but I have no choice. I am drawn towards it like a moth to the light and now it is all I can think of.

Our grief has become a constant longing. Mummy rarely gets up from the settee and her cheeks are sunken and grey. She will only eat soup and a small piece of pitta bread once a day. The doctor has urged her to eat because her body is starting to eat itself. Apparently a diet of less than 1,000 calories a day results in the body looking inwards for extra nourishment. Mummy's muscles are starting to waste away and she barely has the energy to climb the stairs. I am trying to get her to eat more all the time and she knows she has to go on for Robbie and Horsey but I fear that something inside her has given up.

You know I used to worry about how fast time was going by. I would work out in my head roughly how long I thought I might have left to live and then I would add a few years based upon the fact that my grandfather lived until he was ninety-three. And I only wanted to live as long as possible so I could spend more time with you. Now time has slowed to an arthritic crawl.

I wonder whether this is feeling sorry for myself. Oma says that we will laugh again and that we will find joy in the achievements of Robbie and Horsey and that even our own lives must still be worth while. I know she is right and maybe one day her predictions will come true but I do feel sorry for myself. I have lost the one that I most loved and before you say anything, I love Horsey and Robbie just as much but love manifests itself in different ways and you were my partner, you gave me comfort, you made me laugh, you made me so proud, you made me feel as if my life hadn't been wasted. We were going to open a restaurant together and you were going to be the chef and I was going to be the elderly waiter. I was going to come to your opening night in the West End.

I was going to walk you up the aisle. How can I not feel sorry for myself?

I am trying to be strong. I go through the motions. I walk to the shop. I talk to Craig and Mags and still make them laugh now and again. I answer the phone. I deal with the household problems and I try to find the money we need to survive. But inside I am broken.

Sleep well, my angel.

I love you.

Daddy

Sweetheart,

The weekend has gone by. Paul and Mel came round again on Saturday and they managed to persuade us to go to the pub. It wasn't too hard a decision to make. Robbie had six friends to stay and spent the whole afternoon practising with the band in his room. The noise was deafening but they are really beginning to sound good. Only Charlie McP's bizarre vocals jar my ageing ears.

We eventually made it to the Swan at around 6 p.m. and for some reason I went mad. I drank four pints in less than an hour and then we walked back home and I drank a bottle of whisky with Paul. By 9 p.m. I was being violently sick in the downstairs loo. Mummy said that I looked like a 300-year-old man whose spine had been removed. She's not normally that flattering. I fell asleep on the sofa bed in the computer room and didn't wake up until midday yesterday. I don't have to tell you how I felt and still feel today.

Paul and Mel, whose generosity and compassion seem to have no bounds, invited us to their house to have something to eat. It was raining and bleak, a grim Sunday afternoon, and I had already somehow driven Robbie to Newport to be with Cheese. The house was quiet and we were eager to leave. Horsey came too with his PSP and we found ourselves being pampered by candle light. Paul had made a truly delicious vegetable lasagne with new potatoes cooked in sesame seed oil and baked parsnips. Even Mummy ate a proper helping. It was the most food I have seen her eat.

Mel talks about you incessantly. She misses you as much as if you had been her daughter too. Beck writes extraordinary poems about you and posts them on the internet. Her most recent is entitled 'The Dwarf and the Angel' and it is heartbreakingly beautiful. I don't think any of us had any idea how important you and Beck were to each other or that you used to drink red wine in her room and talk about boys. It is not for parents to know the secret lives of their children and I thought I knew everything about you. I am glad that I didn't. Robbie Gladwell, whom we haven't seen for about month, said that you had been on your way to meet a boy in Cambridge and that his name began with W. We found out that you and Livvy were going to meet Woody. How Robbie Gladwell knew that or guessed remains beyond my understanding.

I don't have a copy of 'The Dwarf and the Angel' but Beck wrote this poem for you and read it out at your service.

Charlie:
I'd hear your laughter before I saw you
Envious of those rustic red curls
Golden sprinkles across a porcelain nose

Exquisite ivory innocence
Taller than me
As you like to remind me
And wise beyond your years
I hope you know how proud I was
When you waved at me in corridors
You could get away with anything
That mischievous glint in your eyes was irresistible
Like chocolate which we loved to eat and whisper
I told you all my secrets
Like a best friend
I forgot you were younger than me
But it didn't really matter
You could make me forget
Everything was funny
You fell asleep in my bed
Watching button moon
And it reminded me of your button nose
I teased you about boys at school
You thought they were all silly
And I agreed
You dressed in my clothes
And you always looked beautiful
I remember we spent all evening
Preparing dance routines to the Spice Girls
Lay on the trampoline
And laughed until we couldn't breathe
I told you ghost stories in the fields
Because you begged me to
Then you got scared

And we played hide and seek
Retreated into makeshift worlds
Amongst the bushes and under the stars
We planned how we could make the grown ups stay
    longer
So we could stay up all night
I often tried to imagine how beautiful you would
    become
It seemed almost inconceivable
The hearts you would capture
But you will always have mine
And I know you can never be forgotten.

Rebecca Bowe

I didn't realise how close Beck and Miles feel to us. Miles has barely spoken to me and yet I have known him for ten years, but there is a warmth in his greeting and the way he shakes my hand that speaks louder than words. Beck, on the rare occasions that we bump into her when she is back from university, hugs me with a barely concealed ferocity. Paul and Mel are rightly proud of them and I am proud of them too. My regret is that Miles and Robbie are no longer the inseparable friends they once were but they are talking again and I notice a gradual coming back together. I know we are lucky to have such good friends.

It is the middle of Monday afternoon. Andy is finishing the floor in the kitchen for which he refuses to accept any money. You would love it. It is shiny and very slippery

and you would be sliding up and down it and probably
sleeping on it. It is certainly clean enough to eat off. I am
going to have the house valued in the next couple of days
and then the whole process of moving will begin again.
Mummy has roused herself to do some painting for which
I am very grateful. She is so much better at it than me.

I went to Sudbury to see Oma this morning. She has
framed two fantastic photographs of you. One was taken
when Mummy took you to see the ballet in Covent
Garden and the other is of you in a ragged T-shirt with
no sleeves, taken when you were about eight. I found just
looking at the pictures unbearable and I couldn't stop the
tears. Oma cuddled my head as I sat and she stood over
me. We were both crying. I don't know whether now is
the worst time. It is certainly worse than it was. If things
are to get worse still, perhaps I will not be able to go on.
I miss you constantly. Last night a new series of *24* began.
To watch it without you seemed like a heresy but watch
it we did. Afterwards no one spoke and I made some tea
and soon we just lay down and went to sleep.

I have been trying to sort out the finances so that we
can pay the bills and not go too much further into debt. I
went to the job centre in Braintree on Friday afternoon.
I was there for more than an hour, stripped bare before a
melancholy young woman called Mrs Sansom. You have
to tell them everything. I told them that I am a forty-
eight-year-old man who has lost his daughter, has a
business that doesn't work, huge debts that are only
surmountable if we sell our house, little prospect of a
proper job because for some reason I am unemployable,

and a questionable will to go on. Because Mummy earns the colossal sum of £415 per month we are not eligible for income support or help with our council tax. We can claim incapacity benefit which will provide us with a maximum of £80 per week. Should we get this, and it is by no means certain, we will have between us nearly £900 a month. That is less than the mortgage and the council tax on their own. I pointed this out to Mrs Sansom who regarded me mournfully and said that she was sorry. I must get a job and quickly but I am frightened to leave Mummy on her own. I realise now that I do not have a choice.

Uncle Davy just called me. He is in Portsmouth with Auntie Trish visiting Trish's brother Dennis. Typically I had no idea where he was. I remember once we were in Danny's Bar together and Davy said that he was just popping out to the baker's to get a Danish pastry. I didn't see him for three days. He had decided on a whim to go to London. It must be hell being married to him. Anyway he wants me to work tomorrow because he can't. Luckily it's half term and Robbie and Horsey will be here to keep Mummy company. I think I told you some time ago that I had been to London once in the van to pick up a container load of cheese and some tapas from Products of Spain. Tomorrow will be my first time in the van doing a delivery run. I know that you would be with me but I will still have to get behind the wheel and set off into the dark with an empty seat beside me. It will be the same run, the same chefs, the same pubs and everybody there knows what has happened. I will try to smile and the chefs will be incredibly sympathetic and ask me how I am getting on, and some may even tell me how much they miss you. And I will set down the tray of olives that I have been carrying on the nearest worktop, hand over the invoice and make my way back to the van without you.

I can remember most vividly the last time we drove together up to the Falcon near Fotheringhay. You had never been there before and I was really excited because I knew you would love Fotheringhay and I told you all about it long before we actually got there. I think you thought that I was exaggerating, telling you about this tiny village that exists completely out of time, stuck in Cromwell's England, its huge, austere church towering over the surrounding countryside, the place where Mary, Queen of Scots, was beheaded, with sheep grazing right up to the church doors, and giant crows or maybe even ravens, perching on the stone gargoyles and leering down at us from the battlements. I think the church frightened you a bit. It certainly frightened me. But you loved the river.

Just as we were leaving, driving over the quaint little humpbacked bridge, leaving the terrifying church behind us, you gazed out at the river and said that we should stop and did we have time to go for a walk. Of course it was the most beautiful afternoon. We parked by a five-bar gate and climbed over into the field and you ran to the water's edge and I ran after you. It was perfect. No people, no cars, no pylons, no sounds of any kind. The river slept in the heat of the sun and not a single ripple disturbed its surface. The river bank ran in a straight line for about a quarter of a mile and then curved sharply to the right under a stand of chestnut trees. You said you'd race me to the river bend and set off without waiting for an answer. I knew then that it would be impossible to be happier than I was at that moment. And it didn't matter that I was only a van driver and we had no money and we couldn't afford to go on holiday. I had the most beautiful daughter who found joy in the simplest things and loved to be with her father. That was five months ago and then the world ended.

It's late now, nearly ten at night. Mummy is watching skating on the television. She has been painting ever since Andy left. Something has changed in her. Today she has quietly gone about her business, cleaning and cooking, reading the paper. We do not talk much, after all what is there to say, but I stroke her back and she will take my hand and squeeze it. Horsey is staying out for the night with Jonny. Suzanne rang at 7 p.m. and asked whether it would be OK. I must fetch Robbie in about half an hour. This is our first evening on our own. We shared a tin of soup and I ate a piece of bread and butter. I cannot think of anything but you. There is no future, nothing to look forward to.

I love you so much. Sleep well. I'll come up and see you, I promise.

Daddy

Hello, darling,

I went to work this morning for Uncle Davy just as I said I would. I left Mummy and Robbie sleeping and crept out of the house. It was raining again and I switched on the radio for company as I made my way to Sudbury. When I am alone now I feel that I am walking a tightrope strung between two worlds and like a tightrope walker I must control my breathing and keep my balance or I will fall.

I think in my simplistic way that the two worlds are the past and the future. You inhabit the past. Images of you flicker constantly through my mind, the sound of your voice and the strange array of noises that you would make when you didn't feel that words were necessary. Dismissive grunts, snuffles and half-laughs to indicate disapproval or delivered in response to an unfunny joke. A perfect image of you in your bathing suit hurtling down the water slide at Cambridge swimming pool whilst I am waiting at the bottom ready to catch you. I can feel your slippery body, like an eel, one moment in my arms and then you are gone, laughing, running back to go again. From the top of the stairs you would shout down to me, 'Watch me, Daddy.' I couldn't take my eyes off you.

The future world is a place that I cannot imagine. If I fall into it I will have to go on without you. It is a place where I am frightened that my memories of you might fade and that there will be times when I don't think of you. I want to fall into the past and find myself gathered up in your arms, a place where I can be with you for ever. But for now I am on my tightrope, breathing deeply, just trying to put one foot in front of another to the end of each day, always knowing exactly what the next day will bring. It's like running a marathon that never ends.

I have just returned from Newport with Robbie and Cheese. It is not too late for once and I am tempted just to lie down and go to sleep. We followed the full moon home, throwing its cold winter light through cracks in a glacier of cloud. I remember how I told you so little time ago that before I die I want to stand on the moon and look down on the earth and, above all, I wanted you to be there with me. We were going to stand side by side in our spacesuits, two inconsequential humans suddenly aware of their place in the universe. I still want to keep my dream alive because when I get to the moon I might find you there waiting for me. Don't leave me. I will write again tomorrow.

Bless you, night-night.

Daddy

My angel,

Too much happened yesterday and by the time we eventually returned home at midnight I was far too tired to write.

In the morning Reverend Titford came to see us. Horsey was asleep on the settee so we sat with him in our sparkling new kitchen, surrounded as always by pictures of you. He said much more this time and for me, at least, he was a comfort. He embraces us with his certainty and for the two hours that he spent with us, we both felt that you must indeed be in a better place. He said that nothing could diminish your 'Charlieness'. The part of you that made you you is not lost.

He brought us a book written by others who have suffered a terrible loss, ordinary people and great writers and poets. The famous French author Victor Hugo lost his daughter when she was only nineteen. In the depths of his grief he wrote: 'The children must die so that the grass may grow.' I understand and I do not understand. I understand that he means that death is natural and that we are all part of an endless cycle. I do not understand why the children must die. People try to find comfort in words, pictures, memories, a beloved scarf or brooch, something that was special to the one they loved. Mummy wears your school blazer and I sleep sometimes with your sweater bound around my neck or I use your school clothes for a pillow. At night we fight over who will have your duvet.

After the Reverend left I had to go into Saffron Walden to buy some food. Also we needed some chocolates for a hamper order. I went to the Sceptred Isle delicatessen where we used to go together to choose delicious new things to go in the hampers. Hot vampire relish for the horror hamper, pasta and sun-dried tomatoes and wild mushrooms for the Italian hamper, and those irresistible and yet alarmingly expensive handmade chocolates, which were perfect for any occasion. We had last been to the shop together and you had persuaded me to buy you a tub of enormous green olives, which I knew you wouldn't like, but you said that they were your favourites even though I was almost certain that you had never tasted that kind of olive before, especially as they had whole garlic cloves stuffed into them. We had become friendly with the two ladies who own the shop, Sophie and Nicky, and they had made a tremendous fuss of you and admired your exquisite taste and your almost mystical ability to part me from my money. I was dreading seeing them again. What if they didn't know what had happened? What if they asked after you?

I stepped through the door and turned to my right where the cheese counter is and Sophie saw me. The shop was empty and she came to me immediately, her face collapsing and tears welling in her eyes. I tried to buy some chocolates and a small piece of Parmesan cheese and a slice of home-made quiche that I thought Mummy might eat but she refused to take any money. It was, she said, the least they could do.

On the way home I stopped at the new estate agent in the high street and arranged for a valuation. A man is coming on Monday and we have four days to make the house as presentable as possible.

When I arrived home Mummy had been cleaning the bathroom. I had never realised that the taps were in fact silver as they had always been a dirty yellow colour that I assumed was what happened to brass under the effects of hardened water. No, it was just plain dirt, probably accumulated over the twenty years since the house was originally built. It seems the previous owners were even less houseproud than us.

In the evening I took Robbie to see another band at the Portland Arms. That's two bands in less than a week. He told me that he had been waiting for more than a year to see this band but we arrived half an hour late and we missed them. It's the first time that a band has performed on schedule in living memory. Sod's law, it seems, is still healthy and determining our lives. Robbie and Cheese stayed to watch the other bands that they didn't want to see anyway and I sat in the bar in my usual place, reading and making a pint of lager shandy last three hours. The government has just passed a law banning smoking in all public places but it won't come into force until next year so I made the most of our remaining freedom and smoked whilst I read and slowly sipped my shandy.

I am reading a book called *Moondust*, which John recommended to me. It is a series of linked interviews with the nine men still living who walked on the moon. Soon all will be gone as the youngest is seventy-three. All of the moonwalkers found their lives profoundly changed by their experience. Three have become devoutly religious, one claiming that he actually heard the voice of God. Another, a man named Edgar Mitchell, underwent an epiphany, a life-changing event in which, in a moment of absolute clarity, he realised that a greater intelligence was at work. He has devoted the rest of his life to trying to find answers. Some of the astronauts were no longer able to function in normal society and dropped out. These men stood on the edge of infinity and they must have realised how alone we really are, just a pinprick of light in an infinite vastness. For them, as it is now for me, it became a necessity to believe in something else because if there is no God, no grand design, no purpose, then humanity is alone, adrift on a spinning ball of iron on an eternal sea.

I know you used to think that I loved Robbie the most. It isn't true. I've always told myself that I love all three of you equally and I hope that I am not fooling myself. Robbie is our first-born and I think there is always something desperate about a father's relationship with his eldest son. I did everything first with Robbie and because of that it may have seemed to you, and maybe to Horsey as well, that he came before either of you in my affections. You were, you ARE, my daughter. My only daughter. To me almost indescribably beautiful and, as you grew older, you opened yourself up to those around you, the most perfect rose unfolding her petals for the world to see.

So little time has gone by and I find myself failing to come to terms with the idea of life without you. I keep thinking of ways to make what happened unhappen and for a lot of the time I carry on as if in a dream from which I am desperate to wake up. The days go by untroubled by your laughter and with each new morning I find myself diminished.

I love you so much. You will never leave me and I will never leave you.

Daddy

My darling Charlikins,

I worked again for Uncle Davy. It was 'the Huntsbridge run' as he calls it and you and I had last made all the deliveries on that route together. I had a maximum of twelve drops meaning at least six hours on the road, six hours alone in that van, six hours to think only of you.

I went to Fotheringhay. The sun shone as before and a slight breeze ruffled the surface of the water as the river passed under the bridge. I stopped where we had stopped and looked out across the meadow. I could see you running, your magnificent auburn hair streaming out behind you. I stood, leaning against the gate, unashamed of my tears, barely able to breathe. Three swans studiously ignored me, seeming to find more interest in a singular water lily. Perhaps they were just being kind, not wishing to intrude on my grief. Sometimes when I am alone I scream your name aloud, something basic inside me venting its fury at the cruelty, the injustice, the horror in the world.

When I got back to the warehouse, one of the Kosovan refugees who cleans cars on the forecourt asked me for a lift into Sudbury. His name is Bash, which must be short for something like Bashir, or maybe he's called Bash because he bashes people up. He's young, mid–twenties, I would guess, with a sad but noble face and very quiet. He asked me how we all were. I said that we were OK. Some days were more tolerable than others. I suggested to him that he cannot have had the easiest of lives and he nodded, still looking straight ahead. I said that since we had lost you, I had become more aware of how much suffering there is in the world and that I knew that there were many, many people who suffered like us. Then he looked at me. 'Yes, many,' he said, 'and many who have suffered more.'

I've just got back from picking up Robbie. He has been recording three songs at a friend's house in Saffron Walden. Mummy is going out tonight with Mel Bowe to a music festival in Bishop's Stortford. She doesn't want to go but she doesn't want to stay at home either. Over the last two weeks she has changed, not in her demeanour but she appears to have realised that life goes on with or without her and she has chosen to play a bigger part. For me, the more that I can do, the less I am left alone with my thoughts. If I am painting or cooking or driving, or going to and fro to ferry Robbie about, at least I have something to distract me. I think Mummy has come to the same conclusion. It is better to be doing something. Also Mummy is eating a little more, probably because she is burning up some energy. She has added an occasional biscuit and cheese to her diet of soup and pitta bread.

We have no money. Mummy doesn't feel that she can go back to work and when and if she feels ready, I don't think she will be able to go back to the school. I still don't feel that I can leave her, not for a whole day anyway. It has been easier this week because of half-term but next week we will be alone again. Because the school are paying Mummy sick pay we are not eligible for any income support. We could get something called incapacity benefit but then I couldn't work at all and I would rather work when I can for Uncle Davy. Selling the house is our only chance. Oma is beside herself with worry as well as grief. She told me yesterday that she has nothing left to look forward to. That without you there will be no more joy in her life. Perhaps if I can show her that we will be all right and that we will have enough money to survive, she will have one less worry and that may be of some comfort to her.

Nothing changes. I love you. I will always love you. Night-night, my darling.

Daddy

Sweetheart,

Another day has nearly passed. It is eight in the evening and Robbie has been working in his room, at least he says he has. He must finish an English essay by tomorrow as part of his coursework for the GCSE.

Horsey has been to a party at the barracks in Wimbish. I went to pick him up and spent ten minutes talking to the father of the boy whose party it was. A nice man with a strong, open face. He is a soldier and has served two tours of duty fighting in Iraq. Although we had never met before, he was aware of what had happened and he asked after Mummy and Robbie. I said that we were all right, that we face the days one at a time, not thinking far into the future. Sometimes a kind of numbness envelops us and allows us to function, and at other times the misery engulfs us and we cannot believe that such a thing could happen. He nodded. His job naturally helps him to acclimatise better to the idea of death.

One of the boys at the party lost his father two years ago, killed by a mine in Baghdad. The news was on the television in the background. A landslide in the Philippines killed 1,800 people sometime on Saturday. A whole school was buried with more than a hundred children inside. A hundred sets of parents, a hundred mothers and fathers united in their grief and their horror, just another day to the rest of the world. I keep saying the same thing, that there is no comfort in the suffering of others, but there is something. A sense of not being alone, of not being singled out and, like so many others, our family has been shown the true nature of existence. Life really does hang by a thread and we can be snuffed out in the blink of an eye. We are like ants, unaware of the oncoming tread of a heavy boot. So why bother planning for the future if the future is so precarious? We have to, we have no choice. We either go on or we give up.

I haven't done much today. Grief is hard work. It sits on my shoulders like a great grey rock and wraps itself around me like a heavy cloak. Sometimes just getting up is as much as I can do, trudging to the kitchen, going through the charade of making tea, trying to read the paper but for me the anger and resentment are always there, simmering just below the surface.

The Sunday supplements lie strewn across the kitchen table. I am drawn to the trivial, the self-important, things to feed my anger. Elton John suffers great distress because the *Sunday Times* calls him rude and arrogant. The actress Halle Berry sinks into depression because she catches her husband sleeping with someone else. A woman sues her local council after getting her toe caught under a park bench.

I hate these people and yet maybe, in another life, a life that ended less than three months ago, I would have found some sympathy, imagined myself in a similar situation. But really it is the normality that I hate. Life goes on. The world barely pauses for breath whilst we scream and rage. People go to work, they gather around the water cooler, they travel on the tube, they get drunk, they make love, and for a day or a week the horror that befalls a family engages their interest, even keeps them awake at night as they imagine death knocking at their own door.

It is late now. We have just been watching *24*. Mummy and Horsey and I all lay together on the floor under a duvet. Horsey was in the middle, cracking his fingers and talking through all the most important bits. He does it on purpose to see how far he can push me before I get angry. I am not angry with him. I am tense and hollow and full of longing. As I lay on the floor I put out my right arm and cuddled you even though you were not there. I pulled you close to me, buried my nose in your hair and felt you swing your leg over mine, always resting the heaviest part of your leg on the most sensitive part of my shinbone. You rested your foot on top of my foot and tried to interlock our toes and then you turned over and snuggled into me, sucking your thumb with your eyes closed. 'Love you, Daddy,' you would say. I love you, darling.

I stood in the kitchen, leaning against the work surface, smoking a cigarette. Mummy came to stand with me. We didn't speak. As much as it is possible to know, we are feeling the same. This is our life now. It is not going to change. There won't be a phone call to tell us you will be coming home. We won't wake up tomorrow and find you snoring gently in your bed. This is our life. A life without you. I can't stand the helplessness. I can't stand not being able to do anything. The future is a no man's land of pain and sorrow and longing.

I will dream of you and cuddle you.

Night-night.

Daddy

Good morning, my angel,

It is about eleven o'clock. I can hear the dustman outside collecting the rubbish. Mummy is still asleep on the settee. She had a terrible night. She was still awake at 5 a.m. I slept fitfully, getting up to go to the loo at least twice and suffering a sneezing fit. I found Mummy sitting at the computer playing solitaire, her pale face given a ghostly hue by the dim blue light thrown out from the computer screen.

Robbie is at home too. We had a terrible row and although I drove him to school, he was so upset that it was pointless to try to make him go. I think he would probably have spent the whole day sitting on a bench in the churchyard if I had left him. He won't get up in the morning and I have to nag him constantly. There is nothing new there as you will know. Eventually he shuffled into the kitchen at a quarter past eight, moaning and grumbling under his breath. Horsey was already up and dressed and arranging his hair in the bathroom. He has grown his fringe so that it completely covers his face. I can imagine what you would say if you could see him. 'Get a grip, Harry, you're losing it.' Anyway I ignored Robbie for a while but the moaning intensified so I said quietly, 'I know you don't want to go to school, but it's important.'

He just lost it. 'Why do you think I don't want to go to school?' he screamed.

'Because you're moaning,' I said. 'Because it's obvious.'

It didn't take much then before we were shouting at each other. We both said some things that we shouldn't have. Above all, I felt sorry for Horsey, listening to it all, seeing the tears. He is a remarkable little bloke and I love him so much. I did say some bad things to Robbie. I forget that he is sixteen and that he carries a terrible burden just as we all do. He said that I have no idea how he feels and that he has a list of problems as long as his arm and school is the least of them. He can't bear the fact that I don't trust him to do his GCSE coursework. He says that he knows what he is doing and that he will do it. I don't know what he will do if he doesn't get into the sixth form. Perhaps I shouldn't worry. It is enough that we get through each day but I am a natural worrier. I am my mother's son just as you are my daughter. We take the best and the worst from each other.

Most of the day has gone by now. I painted the utility room which was disgusting. The room was disgusting before I painted it and just painting it was a disgusting job. Do you remember? It was the most foul yellow-ochre colour, covered in strange psychedelic smears. Some of the colour shows through after three coats of brilliant white. I often wonder about the people who used to live in this house, whether they painted it the way they did on purpose or whether they had been brainwashed by some strange cult devoted to primary colours and Victorian chandeliers. After painting the utility room, I went out into the garden and raked the lawn, and after that I found some blunt shears and cut back all the dead flowers in that triangular flower bed by the front door. It began to rain as I hacked away at a rhododendron bush, cold, spiteful rain spitting at my neck and on to the backs of my freezing hands.

I saw you today. I can see you now. When I picked up Horsey from school, you were leaning against the wall by the main gates just as you used to, wearing that look that said, 'Well? You're late. Where have you been?' You must have learnt it from one of your teachers because it made me feel as if I'd just been given a detention. You had on your black tights and that tartan skirt, flat shoes, most likely the ones I bought you in New Look, your blue school sweater and you were wearing your hair in a ponytail. As I pulled up alongside Horsey I could see you looking at me, tapping the dial of your watch. 'You're three minutes late,' you would say before hurling your bag into the back of the car and taking your rightful place in the front seat. You would kick off your shoes and put your feet on the dashboard and lean your head against the window, your thumb firmly in your mouth.

I go to the school every day. I see all the children, your friends, standing together swapping stories, laughing, whispering, pointing at boys. I still search for you as I wait by the zebra crossing. I let the children cross and you are not there. Some days are worse than others. On some days I grit my teeth and my mind goes blank. I pick up Horsey and I make it home and I am OK. Today was unbearable. I could see you. I could hear your voice. You were there but I could not touch you and when I looked, the seat beside me was empty. I fear that I am not doing very well.

I will write again soon. Night–night, sleep tight.

Daddy

Charlie,

Can you hear me? Are you watching me as I type? The last two days have been bleak with despair. I think Mummy has slipped back or, worse, gone deeper into a place that even she didn't realise existed. The man is coming to value the house tomorrow. He was going to come on Monday but we were not ready.

Yesterday and today Mummy has been clearing up, making the bedrooms look tidy. She has been in your room, looking through your books, finding stories that you had written, old birthday cards, letters to your friends or to us after an argument. She has been sorting through your clothes. I don't know how she has found the courage to do it and I fear that these acts have forced her to look directly at the truth. You are not coming back. It's not just that her face is gaunt, it is the hopelessness in her eyes. She doesn't want me to comfort her and there is nothing I can say. If I speak to her she answers in a monotone. She rarely looks at me. Last night I found her crying silently, alone in the living room. I knelt beside her and took her hand and my tears came and I couldn't stop them.

There are more pictures of you on the mantelpiece.
One when you were nine or ten standing outside the
back door at Debden Green with Oma and Auntie
Franky. It was the time when Oma tried to dye her hair
blonde. At first I thought that you were her, wearing a
clown's wig and some kind of prosthetic mask. No human
being should have hair like that. There is another of you
with Robbie and Horsey, wearing army helmets and
standing in front of a military jeep. I don't remember
when it was taken but you were all very young.

Mummy is creating a photographic record of each stage
of your life. I find it strange. I can only think of you as
you were during the last year. I can recall almost every
day. I can replay whole conversations in my head but I
can't seem to go back further than a year. When I try to
remember things that happened at Debden or Stansted, all
I see are still images of you. I cannot bring them to life. I
want to be able to relive every second of your life. I want
to be able to pick any moment at random and just be
with you.

Life has become a long, dark road. Looking back, I
think the shock has lasted almost until now. The human
mind protects itself with adrenalin and wraps itself in layers
of make-believe. For the first month we were surrounded
by friends and family. Now we are mostly alone. When
we sit down to eat, you are not there. When we watch a
film together, you are not there. When I drive, every road
I go down, every view, reminds me that you are not
there. I am not far from madness. I think about going to
sleep and not waking up and being released from this

misery. Tonight I thought about saying to Mummy that I would understand if she wanted to go to you; that I would stay and look after Horsey and Robbie. I didn't say it and I won't say it but I thought it.

I went to work again today. The same delivery run although I was spared Fotheringhay. The Falcon has enough olives and cream cheese to be going on with. I listened to the radio because I do not trust the silence. In the afternoon I suffered a discussion between the authors of self-help books. *A Spiritual Guide to a Better Life*. Be the most that you can be. Everybody can have it all, it's just a matter of self-confidence. Life coaches. Learn to manage your debt. Release your inner self. I listened to the authors argue between themselves. The life coach thought the spirit guide was a phoney. The debt manager doubted the wisdom of suggesting that everybody could have it all. I felt like an alien eavesdropping on a conversation from another dimension.

Another car bomb went off in Iraq today. Twenty-two people were killed and twenty-eight were seriously injured. The newsreader made it sound like a football score. Here in England we don't expect to die before our allotted time, however long that may be, certainly more than the traditional threescore years and ten. We are not really religious so we worship ourselves and devote our lives to making ourselves feel better. If we have too much money, we give some of it away or we work in a soup kitchen on a Saturday night. If we have too little money, we buy a self-help book or we complain that our lives are unfair.

Uncle Stu sent me a text today. He urged me to 'be strong'. I will be strong, my darling.

I love you so much.

Sleep well.

           Your Daddy

My angel,

The man from the estate agent's has been. The house will go up for sale officially in two weeks.

I had another row with Robbie this morning. It has made things worse between Mummy and me. She thinks that he should go to school only if he feels up to it, that whatever happens, the most important thing is that he feels loved. She is right. I am tortured by the fear that he will throw away his life and yet I know how difficult it is for me just to get up in the morning. The enormous effort required to go to work or complete a simple, mundane task. It must be the same for Robbie and for him to be at school, seeing your friends walking down the corridor, peering into classrooms where once you would have been sitting, knowing that each morning when he wakes up that you won't be there, must be unbearable. It is unbearable for us. Horsey goes on, stoically doing what needs to be done. Is he protected by the innocence of youth or is he stronger than us?

Auntie Jill arrived this evening. She rang to say that she would be here at five so we didn't even begin to expect her until eight. You can imagine how shocked we were when she turned up at seven. We were completely unprepared. She brought with her almost the entire contents of the local Tesco's store. The fridge is bulging like Pavarotti's trousers. I don't know who will eat it all. Robbie ate a bowl of chilli and so did I. Mummy had a cup of soup and a crispy chicken leg. Horsey had sausages, beans and waffles. That left a family-sized lasagne, two bags of prepared salad, six pounds of potatoes and an assortment of breads and cakes for Auntie Jill. She is a wonderful distraction. On the surface she behaves as if nothing has happened. She is very businesslike. There is only one of her and yet within minutes the house seems to be full of noise and life where before there had been silence and a kind of living death. She barks orders from the kitchen, simultaneously peeling carrots whilst talking to Patrick or Toby on the phone. She is perpetually busy and I would do anything to get her to move in with us. She hums with life and I realise more than ever why you loved her so much.

Mummy and Auntie Jill have been talking in the kitchen. Robbie, Horsey and I have been watching something on television in which the main plot line concerned an elderly lady dying of Alzheimer's disease. She was giving evidence in a trial and was ruthlessly exposed by the defence lawyer as an unreliable witness. I lay on the floor with my back against the settee. Robbie lay next to me although he is too old to want to cuddle me now and I'm not sure I want to cuddle him. He is very bony and his feet smell.

Everything is tainted by your absence. As the story unfolded before us I was taken back to the time when

Mummy's mother was dying of Alzheimer's and we would go down every weekend to see her in that grim hospital in Poole. You were four years old and yet you insisted on coming into the ward when Robbie stayed outside, probably looking after Horsey who was still confined to his pram. Your only concern was to give some comfort to Mummy's Oma whom you would find sitting in a threadbare armchair, smelling faintly of urine and disinfectant, her once open and inquisitive face turned inward and twisted by whatever demon, intent on stealing her memory and ultimately her life. You weren't afraid. You climbed on to her lap and gave her your love even though she no longer knew who you were. Sometimes something flickered in her eyes and a desperate, half-remembered smile passed across her lips. That was you. That was how you were. You always gave all of yourself to others.

With my Oma you were the same. You always came with me to see her although sometimes boredom got the better of you and you would employ underhand tactics to disrupt our conversations or draw attention to yourself. Drumming your fingers on the table or playing the piano very loudly or accidentally on purpose tripping over as you gallumphed aimlessly through the house. Oma used to get very irritable with you but she is eighty-three. But most times you would be a joy. In the summer we sat on Oma's tiny patio and built her flatpack garden furniture and then you mowed the lawn. She made you vast glasses of orange squash and gave you suspicious cakes that had passed their sell-by dates. Afterwards we would go to

Danny's Bar and you would revel in the fuss that the staff made over you and sit drinking non-alcoholic cocktails with all the maturity of a worldly-wise eighteen-year-old.

Sometimes I wonder why I am writing these letters. What are my motives? Am I writing to keep you alive or to keep a record of all the things that you did and the times we spent together? I think that for the most part I am trying to help myself, to keep in contact with you, not to let you go. Where I used to read books purely for the escapism they provided, I have found myself drawn to books that explore the outer limits of human experience and books which, I hope, may provide an insight into beliefs and possibilities that will help me to keep believing that you still exist in some way. I am not capable of the leap of faith required to find comfort in a guaranteed afterlife. Not yet at any rate. But I have always been fascinated by the sheer impossibility of our existence. Not long ago we went to see the film of *The Hitch Hiker's Guide to the Galaxy*. I don't think you thought it was that great and nor did I, to tell the truth, but as a student I had fallen in love with the books and one line in particular, which I have clung to down the years. 'In an infinitely improbable universe, the infinitely improbable is as probable as anything else.'

In the book that the Reverend Titford gave us, there is a passage written by a mother who had lost her child. It is heartbreaking and yet ultimately life-affirming. She says that after three months she had reached a point where she no longer wanted to go on. The business of living had become 'disagreeable'. It is a strange word to use, a stoic word. I would not call what I feel disagreeable. It will be twelve weeks on Saturday and for me the business of living is a burden. I know what tomorrow will bring.

I love you. I will carry you with me for ever and your light will never dim.

Your Daddy

Hello, my angel,

I haven't written for a few days. I am sorry. I have
been with you or you have been with me for all my
waking moments and, I hope, also while I slept.

Auntie Jill left yesterday afternoon. It has been hard to
find the time to write while she has been with us
because she spends much of her time on the computer
checking her bank details or ordering curtain material
from trendy shops in Cheshire. Because she comes
infrequently and it is so uplifting to have her with us, I
can hardly complain when she seeks to relax by sitting in
front of this screen.

Since I last wrote, I worked again for Uncle Davy. I
found myself doing the same delivery run that I had done
on that day. I did not want to do it and although the sun
shone and the countryside sparkled with the freshness of
promised spring, it was almost unendurable. I was forced
to replay each moment of the horror. Perhaps the worst
thoughts came as I returned to the places that I had visited
in ignorance, struggling in with ten-kilo tubs of olives and
swapping banter with chefs even after you had departed
this world and I still knew nothing. I think I found out
the truth at about three in the afternoon, over four hours

afterwards. I cannot reconcile that lost time. I remember calling in at the Ship at Levington at midday and falling foul of the chef because the pesto sauce had gone off. Already more than an hour after the accident. I was so upset by the pesto sauce that I offered to drive into Ipswich to find some more, panicking that we might lose an account because of some itinerant mould.

I have been searching for the right word to describe how I feel. Torment. I am tormented by memories, tormented by your absence, tormented by helplessness and guilt. I promised that I would never say 'what if' or 'if only' but the mind and the body do not always respond to reason. If only I had spent more time teaching you about the dangers of crossing the road and, by extension, railway crossings. If only I had forced you to come to work with me or taken the time off so that I could have driven you to Cambridge instead.

None of this will bring you back and yet I still find myself searching for ways to change the past. The rational part of me tells me that this is because I still haven't accepted your death. I am shocked that I have been able to type the word. I know that I am unable to say it. I may never be able to say it. To say it is to admit the truth. Perhaps just writing the word is part of the so-called 'healing' process. The books that I have been reading all say that acceptance comes before healing. What is healing in this context? I will never look forward to tomorrow. I know that I will laugh. I laugh now. I laughed yesterday. Laughing is what humans do. It is a spontaneous reaction. A person does not need to be happy to be able to laugh.

I have become somebody else. I look the same. I
sound the same. Somewhere deep within me I have a
similar sense of humour to the person who used to be
me. I am not Mummy or Robbie or Horsey and I
cannot, for certain, know what goes on in their minds
or the details of their private nightmares, but I am sure
that they have all become different people too. We fell
into a river of grief and we have been borne along by
the current, screaming and struggling, sometimes going
under. The river has no end except perhaps in a sea of
melancholy where we might float for ever. I fear that I
am becoming used to being in the river. I struggle less,
knowing that there is no escape. I am becoming an
observer. The old world, which once I was part of,
where there is happiness and hope, only exists for me as
a two-dimensional image, a picture that is becoming less
real. I listen to the radio, watch television, read the
papers, overhear conversations in shops. 'My daughter is
studying for her A levels. My daughter is going to spend
a year in Africa. My daughter wants to be an actress.
My daughter is going to compete in the 2012 Olympics.
Next year my daughter and I are going to go shopping
in New York.' I hear everything. I lost my daughter.
All the things that we were going to do have turned to
dust.

Although I am your father, I cannot conceive of a
greater love than the love I have for you. My love for
you has no boundaries, no conditions, it is absolute. It
consumes me and leaves me hollow, aching and sick and
desperate. But maybe you are there and all I have to do is

believe that you will always be with me even though I cannot see you. I will try. I will find a way, I promise you.

I love you.

Daddy

Darling one,

I am sorry that I haven't written for a couple of days. Sometimes I sit before the computer screen and my mind goes blank. We are like patients slowly waking up from a coma to find that the most vital part of ourselves has been removed. We slip in and out of nightmarish dreams but to be conscious and awake is worse.

The man came this morning to measure all the rooms in the house and take pictures so that we can finally go ahead with the business of selling. We have been working to clean the house and make it look as good as possible but we have no enthusiasm and no pleasure in the anticipation of the move to come. We cannot stay here. We desperately need the money and the memories are too painful. I do not think that by running away we will escape or that, by our living somewhere else, life will become somehow easier. I have been in your room, sitting on the edge of your bed, hugging your pillow, trying to find the scent of you. Your clothes are cold now but I find some comfort in pressing your school sweater to my face. It is yours, after all. We will take everything with us and throw away nothing. Your Alkaline Trio poster stares down from the wall above your bed. You only put it up the week before the accident. So much of you surrounds us and makes your absence all the more intolerable.

Yesterday I received the final draft of the letter that the solicitors intend to send to Network Rail. I have not given my consent to send it yet. It is four pages long and details twelve instances of alleged negligence on the part of the rail operator. It is written in that leaden legalese that reduces everything to barely comprehensible facts, stripped of emotion. In the letter you have become a statistic. If I agree to send it, the horrible game starts. I have asked Mummy her opinion but she is not really interested beyond her hatred and despair. It is for me to attend the inquiry and the inquest, and go to court if necessary. I know it is far from certain we would win a case against Network Rail. I am only concerned in making the station safer so that some small good may come from your sacrifice.

On the radio I heard the brother of a murdered policeman say that he forgives the killer. The man said that his Christian faith and his belief that Jesus died for our sins gave him the strength to carry on and that, if Jesus could forgive, then so could he. I do not share this faith and I cannot suddenly believe in order to try to make myself feel better. I do not blame a particular person for what happened. I do not blame the driver, who must still be traumatised, or the many thousands of employees, most of whom are probably good and decent people, but I can't forgive the company that has not had the decency to write to us or contact us in any way after more than three months.

Nothing will bring you back. This is our life now. We will survive and the surface of the wound will heal so that others neither know nor notice.

I have just been to the kitchen to make myself a cup of tea. Mummy is in the bath and Horsey is doing his homework in the living room. I think Robbie is working in his bedroom. No, I can hear him playing his guitar. He has got a gig next week in Newmarket, supporting a band called Six Ways from Sunday who have a CD out. He is really excited, at least as excited as I have seen him for some time. The band sound brilliant and Robbie writes really catchy tunes but I fear that Charlie McP's singing could hold them back from greater things. His voice sounds like a bottle top being scraped across a blackboard. Robbie is not fazed. He says Fat Mike from NOFX can't sing and it hasn't prevented them from being successful. Chitson has taken Liam's place in the band, which is good because I like Chitson although for a big lad he wears alarmingly tight jeans. Tight jeans seem to be coming back into fashion. Robbie alone wears his trousers so that the crutch hangs down below his knees. He walks as if he is carrying a small litter of puppies in his boxer shorts. I asked Cheese whether she finds Robbie's style attractive and she said that she thinks he looks really cool. Far be it from me to comment any further.

It's snowing outside, nothing spectacular but snow nonetheless. I don't suppose it will settle. According to some, yesterday was the first day of spring although I subscribe to the belief that spring starts with the equinox on 21 March or is it 22? Either way the mornings and evenings are getting lighter. Little armies of snowdrops are gathering on the grassy banks of the roads into Thaxted, the first obvious sign that nature's annual cycle of rebirth is beginning. If I were a Buddhist I would know now that you had been given new life and that, because you had lived so joyously and been overwhelmingly kind and generous, you would certainly be born into an even better life. I know that I don't have to believe in something for it to be true.

The night before last I suddenly thought that I could smell gas leaking from the fake coal-effect fire in the living room. It was very late or very early, and Mummy and Robbie and Horsey were all asleep. We were in the living room as usual even though the doctor has tried to persuade us to sleep upstairs. It is not an option for us until we move, when we will sleep upstairs unless we find ourselves in a bungalow. The more I lay awake sniffing, the more convinced I became that gas was leaking from the fire. Certainly it would explain why Horsey gets so many headaches. Eventually I got up and found a lighter which I then gingerly held over the gas outlet valve. In my paranoia I was sure that I saw the flame flicker, lose the will to go on and then suddenly flare into life again. I rang the Gas Board first thing in the morning and they told me to open all the windows, turn off the gas at the mains and to try to refrain from smoking until the gas SWAT team arrived. With remarkable efficiency a small light blue Transco van pulled up within an hour. A barrel-chested man of Italian descent, who looked as if he could armwrestle an orang utan, pronounced that the gas levels were within acceptable limits and that there was nothing to worry about.

As he was leaving he saw your pictures lining the mantelpiece and there was something about him that led me to tell him what had happened. He told me that his son had been just sixteen when he had been knocked down and killed by a hit-and-run driver. That had been fifteen years ago. More recently his sister had lost her eleven-year-old son in a car accident. He asked me how you had died and although I find it almost impossible to talk about, because of the man's own tragedies I forced myself to go back again to that terrible day. As I talked the man's eyes filled with tears. When I had finished he told me that his son had been deaf and, although the driver had sounded her horn, she had refused to brake or veer around him. His son simply failed to hear the car and it had ploughed into him at seventy miles an hour. He thought that the woman who had killed his son was guilty of murder and he would never forgive her. We talked longer and he told me about his boat and how he goes fishing with his other son. He said that they go fishing for pike on the Norfolk Broads and he told me how much pleasure it gives him. He is never without the pain, though, or the ache of longing.

And so I found another brother, another member of this awful club. There are so many of us.

As each day goes by I find myself growing restless. I want to do something. I want to just start walking and keep walking until I feel like stopping, or row single-handed across the Atlantic, or climb a mountain on my own. I can't row and I can't climb although I believe that, with the will, anything is possible or almost anything anyway. Recently a man walked from Land's End to John o'Groats completely naked except for his boots. Good luck to him, I say, although he upset some of the more extreme *Daily Mail* readers. I suggested to Robbie that perhaps I could walk naked to John o'Groats or, as it will be my first time, maybe just once around the Lake District. I could practise by walking to Saffron Walden in my slippers. Robbie was horrified. He said that I would be beaten up by armed gangs. I must do something though. I can see how easy it will be to slip back into a routine. Going to work, watching the television, reading the occasional book. Everything will be the same but different. I cannot allow that to happen.

Mummy and I are going to walk up to the church now and light a candle for you. We are going to go fully clothed.

It is my curse that I can only love you.

Your Daddy

For the first five years of her life it seemed as if Charlie was never out of
my arms. Why, she said, do I need legs if my daddy can carry me

Charlie is about two in this photograph. It was best to take cover
when she had a weapon in either hand

Charlie asleep on the settee, sucking her thumb, when she was three.
She never stopped sucking her thumb and would get very angry
when certain people suggested that it wasn't a good idea

Robbie, Horsey and Charlie in a rare moment when they weren't attacking each other

In Uncle Davy's garden. Looking at this picture now, it is hard to imagine how happy I must have been

Unlike her brothers, Charlie loved theme parks. Only the highest, fastest, most terrifying rollercoasters would do

On the beach near Wells in Norfolk. Charlie always needed a big stage

Charlie in 1999 when she was seven, getting ready to go to a party

The children in their 'goggles' phase. They also wore them when they went swimming

The Thompson family lost somewhere in Paris in 1999. Shortly after this picture was taken Horsey succeeded in curing the crick in my neck

Charlie with her mother at Covent Garden in 2002, when they went to see the Russian ballet. At about this time Charlie had perfected what she called her 'bad ballet' following ballet lessons at Elsenham village hall

Charlie's cousins, Dan and Simon, on the occasion of Dan's thirtieth birthday party at the Angel Inn, Stoke-by-Nayland, in September 2004. Three months later Dan died in a car accident near to his home

Charlie in Menorca in 2003 eating an ice cream

Charlie drew this flattering portrait of her father and her uncle during the summer of 2004, probably when we weren't looking and with somebody else's crayons

The Thompson family tree. Not every member of the Thompson family felt that their portrait was entirely accurate. Charlie adored her family and wanted as big a family as possible. There are some people here whom I don't even recognise

Hello, poppet,

It is 5.30 p.m. on Friday afternoon. I have been to
Sudbury to see Uncle Davy and Auntie Trish. I left
Mummy but Adele came while I was out. She brought
home-made pumpkin soup and peanut biscuits from
South Africa. She has just returned from visiting Becka
who lives in Johannesburg with her husband and new
baby. Becka sent us the most beautiful card with a shield
made of feathers on the front. You would love it. She
has invited us to visit her and I am going to try to
persuade Mummy although I do not know where we
will get the money.

I remembered that I had asked Adele to bring back
some earth from the African bush. I'd meant it as a joke
but she presented me with a small tube of 'magic powder',
genuine dust from the veldt, trodden down by the hooves
of antelopes and countless other wild animals. On the
instructions it says that I must take off my shoes and stand
facing the sun. Then I should put a small amount of
powder in the palm of my left hand and make a wish as I
blow the dust away. I should then turn and walk away
without looking back. The sun has gone down now so I
will wait until tomorrow and stand barefoot in the road

and wish for your spirit to be safe and free and beyond pain.

I have just had a call from the lawyers. Yesterday I sent back some amendments to their initial draft of the letter of claim that we intend to send to Network Rail. I told Mummy what the lawyer said and I have left her in the kitchen. If we had any made any progress, if our wounds had been healing even without us noticing, this call has picked off the scab. I feel a despair and misery that is somehow even worse than all that has gone before. I am cold. I cannot ever turn my back on what has happened or walk away from the hatred I feel for Network Rail. I have written to the Prime Minister. I do not know whether he will even read the letter and I am sure that, if he does, it will make no difference but I had to do something.

Tomorrow I am going to write to Network Rail and to the Attorney General. I will not stop until the station has been made safer and some small good has come from your death. I was going to write 'from what has happened' but I can't say that any more. Something in me is making me look without turning away. My fingers are not my own. My thoughts are not my own. Yvonne McPartland has promised to help us organise a petition and set up a charity if we have to, to help towards the legal fees amongst other things. Any money we raise will go towards making the rail network safer, especially for children.

I am going to the local paper on Monday to speak to them about some kind of ongoing editorial support. This is just the sort of thing I need you for. Nobody is better than you. Already you would have designed a poster on the computer and I would not be able to stop you from handing them out in the High Street in Saffron Walden and sticking them under car windscreen wipers. I will fight this battle with you at my side and together we will change the law.

I have started to walk up to the shop again. It has rained for days. I wear my long grey coat, which is out of shape and hangs off my shoulders so that Oma thinks I look like a tramp. I walk past the alley that leads to the windmill and see you running in front of me, hiding behind the wall next to the Baptist church. I stop and buy chips on the corner for Horsey and know that I should be buying them for you too and that you would eat most of them even before we made it home but not without at least one sachet of tomato sauce. If it's dark I look up at the sky and see Orion's Belt which was your favourite constellation, and think of you. The loneliness has seeped into the marrow of my bones. I still hold your hand in the car, see the perfect outline of your jaw, your nose bridged by a band of freckles. I can count the hairs in your eyebrows and feel your hair caught between my fingers. Will it always be like this? Auntie Franky calls you the wind dancer, the gypsy girl.

I love you.

Daddy

Hello, my angel,

The longest time has passed since I have written to you. Five days. I am so tired but that is no excuse. The weekend passed and we were surrounded by friends. Paul and Mel came on Friday and we saw them again on Saturday at the Wiggett's. Jill and Alan invited us all to dinner although in the end we had a takeaway from a very busy Indian restaurant in Bishop's Stortford. It was either that or risk Mrs Wiggett's cooking. She is many things and a wonderful friend but cooking has passed her by. She has neither the patience nor the inclination. She says she can tell when a roast is done when the oven starts to smoke. Her idea of providing canapés is to put an unopened packet of crisps in a bowl. If she informs Alan during the day that she intends to cook in the evening, he stays behind after work and organises a business dinner or makes do with a pie from a stall on Liverpool Street station.

We played a pub quiz game and Alan cheated. John Keeling came too and sat holding court, telling us all about his latest television programme. Evenings when we can go out provide a welcome distraction for Mummy. For a few hours she is spared the relentless misery. I am finding it harder and harder to pretend to be happy but I cannot inflict this pall of grief on others. I go out for a walk or lock myself in the bathroom until I can compose myself or discover the strength to continue a conversation about football or work or the national obsession with Tony Blair.

On Sunday, Uncle Davy arrived out of the blue with Oma and Auntie Trish. Mummy was in the bath and Robbie was upstairs with the remnants of his friends who had all stayed the night before. Horsey was caught watching the television and was persuaded by Oma to play the clarinet. It is impossible with Oma to avoid the issues, and she would or could only talk about your accident and the likelihood that Network Rail will admit responsibility. She has spoken to Uncle Hans who has spoken to his eldest son, young Hans, who works as a lawyer for the Dutch National Bus Company. They believe that we should drop any case against Network Rail because we can't win and it will cause too much distress. I do not understand how I could be any more distressed than I already am and letting Network Rail walk away without a fight is not something that I am able to do. Mummy couldn't cope with this level of conversation and she withdrew into her shell, not speaking to anybody.

Auntie Trish called me later to tell me how awful she thought Mummy looked. I see her all the time and I can notice that she has lost weight and that her face is a mask of despair. Her eyes are red rimmed and moist with tears. I do not know what to do except cuddle her when I can and try to cajole her to eat. She shows amazing strength with Robbie and Horsey and rarely lets her guard drop in front of them. She cooks and washes but a new regime has taken over our lives and there is no joy, no laughter, and the house is quiet.

Robbie is sinking too and I must save him. The school is not doing all that it can to help him. Some teachers simply fail to recognise what has happened as an illness, a debilitation, an impossibility. They put pressure on Robbie and tell him that if he doesn't work harder he will fail his GCSEs. He comes home in tears and says that going to school is the most that he can do. I am proud of him and I tell him that it doesn't matter. We can only survive a day at a time. Last week a teacher pulled him back by the hair when he was trying to go into the cafeteria. I have not complained about it because I do not want to deflect the school from the main issue, which is to support Robbie and build up his confidence. Anyway Robbie has begged me not to say anything, convinced that the teacher in question would react badly and make his life even more difficult. I do not know what is wrong with these people. To some, if you haven't got boils all over your face or your arm in a sling, then there can't be anything wrong with you.

I meet people occasionally who ask me whether I'm feeling better. I don't know what to say to them. I don't want to upset them or burden them with our grief but I cannot say that 'Yes, things are fine, we're much better, thank you. Nearly all the symptoms have cleared up.'

I went to see Uncle Davy on Monday because we had some more hamper orders and I needed to get boxes from the warehouse. We never sell enough hampers to actually make any money but sales at least cover our outgoings on the business, which helps to make me feel slightly less than useless. Uncle Davy is struggling too. He has renamed the company Charlie's Larder and produced huge quantities of headed paper and compliment slips and all the other paraphernalia necessary to bombard his customers with the news. I love him for it and you would be so proud. His fleet of white Transit vans will all be reliveried by the end of the week and soon your name will be synonymous with the finest cheeses, olives and sun-blushed tomatoes the region can buy. He is also going to open a shop opposite Danny's Bar called Charlie's Larder and sell goods to the general public. We are gradually turning Sudbury into a memorial for our lost children. I cannot live with it but I cannot live without it.

Yesterday was Tuesday. I went to see a man called John Doe in Dunmow. You know how Mummy hates Dunmow. She is terrified that she will bump into Mrs Thomas. Personally I quite like the place. Anywhere that throws up a person called Dickon Stainer can't be all bad. One of Mummy's colleagues at the school gave me John Doe's number and I called him last week to set up a meeting. He lost his daughter six years ago. I'm not sure how old she was but I think, from the things that he told me, that she had been nineteen or twenty. A picture of her took pride of place on the window sill by his desk and she looked beautiful and full of life, standing on a ski slope somewhere in France. She had been killed in a car accident on a local road on the way to see her boyfriend in Chelmsford. We talked for two hours and he told me that he could no longer remember the first six months after his daughter died. The time had passed in a blur and he had been incapable of anything. His wife didn't stop crying for a year. Like us, he had not been particularly religious but he had found comfort in the words of his local vicar and now he attends church regularly. He says that without faith life is pointless and that we must keep looking for you and that we must find a way to believe. I do believe in you. I look inside myself and I know that nobody can help me. Only I can find the truth.

The silent network of the bereaved grows around us. I received an e-mail this morning from Tina, Livvy's mother. The strength that she showed at the beginning is crumbling and she finds that she can no longer concentrate and that she cries all the time. She finds comfort in her other daughter, Stevie, and they must fight on alone as she is divorced. We must go and see her and perhaps find some comfort in each other.

I will write again soon. There seems to be so much to do but I achieve so little. It will be your birthday on Friday. Linda is making you a cake and I know Mummy has bought you some presents. We are going to Danny's Bar after school, and Paul and Mel are going to come, and Jill and Alan, and some of your friends. Mummy and I sit at the kitchen table when we are alone, surrounded by your pictures, rarely speaking. The passage of time does not heal.

You are inside me, part of me and I take you everywhere.

I love you so much.

Your Daddy

Angel,

It is your birthday. It is about eleven o'clock in the morning. Mummy got up very early, she couldn't sleep. I heard her in the kitchen whilst it was still dark. Robbie and Horsey both went to school and when I returned from taking them, Mummy had gone back to bed. I will let her sleep. We had talked last night about going to Belchamp this morning to see you but I know you are not there and I do not feel ready. I don't know if I will ever feel ready. We cried for most of the evening. I tried to take Mummy in my arms and comfort her but she has withdrawn and sometimes I feel that she does not notice me.

Later when Robbie came down from his room, he tried to cuddle us both. He put one of his long, spindly arms around my shoulders and buried his head in my neck. I am so proud of him. It is he who needs to be comforted by us. He is wise and strong with a good heart. Horsey lay on the settee watching *South Park* and his occasional laughter cracked the silence, a reminder of you. I fear that it is all too much for Horsey to cope with and so he has shut down a part of his memory. I am terrified that it lies in wait for him, a monster in a cage.

There is much to tell you. Do you remember Mags from the Spar? Her house burnt down and Jim Lamb has kindly let her stay with him until she can find somewhere else to live. Her house was hidden on the corner of that little lane beside Annie's house on the road into Henham. It's where we used to cycle last summer. It was a tiny, white-painted bungalow with a beautifully tended rose garden at the front, and fields at the back stretching away over the hill and down into the valley at Debden. We always used to go on our bike rides on Sundays while Mummy was cooking a roast. Horsey rarely came because he was too busy watching television or playing a video game and Robbie couldn't spare the time. Anyway I'm sure he felt riding a bicycle was beneath him, which was good news because it meant that you could ride his bike, which at least had two fully inflated tyres and handlebars that didn't suddenly collapse every time you braked. I had not thought of our bike rides until now. So many times that I was with you were the best times of my life. We used to cycle to Henham, which always struck me as being quite a long way, a round trip of exactly seven and a half miles.

It was three years ago, while we were still living in Debden Green, when you saw the injured pigeon in the ditch just before Sibleys Lodge. I saw the pigeon too and I had had every intention of riding right by without a second look. I have never been overly fond of pigeons. Something about them scares me. They seem permanently on the verge of exploding. You never discriminated against any living thing. You forced me to stop and told me to go and check whether the pigeon was OK. I remember trying to argue with you but you were adamant and I didn't have a chance. You sat astride your saddle with the haughty look of a disapproving school teacher whilst I ran after the pigeon, which hopped and bumped its way into a patch of stinging nettles.

'I'll never get it now,' I said.

'You will,' you said.

Eventually, much to my amazement, I caught the pigeon and discovered that it had a broken wing, badly broken as I remember, and was covered in blood. 'It's been hit by a car,' I said. 'It's got no hope.'

No and hope was not a combination that worked for you and one look at your face told me that I would have to take the pigeon home. Riding a bicycle with one hand whilst holding a wounded and terrified pigeon with the other is an interesting challenge. I feel quite pleased with myself even now as I recall the successful negotiation of nearly three miles of open road whilst you rode on ahead to warn the others and prepare a box with cotton wool for Toby, because that was the name that you had decided upon even while I had been busy blundering through the nettle patch.

You tended Toby for two weeks while his wing healed and eventually he flew away, although only as far as the roof of the house where he sat by the chimney with the slightly bemused, glassy look preferred by pigeons everywhere. You saved Toby's life and a whole army of Erics, Teds, Freds and Barrys, assorted fish, sparrows, robins and lizards that owe you their second chance.

Why weren't you given a second chance?

Mummy is awake now. Ollie just rang to wish you a happy birthday and Sharon Moore called earlier, as did Chitson's mum and John Keeling and Auntie Trish. We received a card from Suzanne Farr and another from Linda and Mike to go with the cake, which is spectacular. It has your name in pink icing right across the middle and Linda has somehow constructed a pink rose out of icing, which is a work of art. I don't suppose it will last long. I brought the cake home last night and had to stand guard to prevent Robbie from desecrating it.

Mike now works in Barclays Bank in Saffron Walden and he keeps a picture of you on his desk. He is a remarkable man. He told me that you have made him a better person and when people come into his office to complain about their lot in life, he tells them about Mummy and me and Uncle Davy and Auntie Trish, and how, in one year, we have lost both you and Dan. He says that you helped to put his life into perspective and that he is more patient with people and finds more time for his own children. You changed so many people's lives because there was no malice in you and you found everything and everybody interesting. You smiled at strangers in the street, at old ladies and small children, you drove away the dark clouds and made the sun shine.

We are going to your party soon when Paul and Mel arrive. A whole horde of yours and Robbie's friends are coming. Chitson and Penny and Charlie McP and Cheese and Fleetwood. Miles is coming too, which has pleased

Horsey because Miles is his new best friend although I expect it is news to Miles. You'd better get ready too, after all, it's your party. Will you sit in the front with me? Bless you.

Daddy

Hello, pops,

It is six o'clock on Sunday evening. I am absolutely shattered. I have spent most of the day writing a business plan for Moviehampers. Do you remember that television programme, *Dragons' Den*? You made me apply to go on it last September. A woman rang from the BBC to tell me that I have a screen test next Thursday for the next series but I need to e-mail her a business plan tomorrow. I think she assumed I had a business plan. I didn't when she rang. I do now although whether it's the sort of business plan that will impress a panel of millionaire entrepreneurs remains to be seen. John says that you have made it happen and I have to make it on to the show for you. All I can say is that I will try. I should be excited but all I can think of is how horrified you would be by the idea of having to watch your father humiliate himself on television. You would be shrieking with delight, ringing up all your friends and arranging a sleepover for the night in question, telling me what to wear and how I should have my hair cut and that unfortunately there wouldn't be enough time to lose my double chin but perhaps they would be able to hide my nose in make-up. I think you would agree that dyeing my hair would be a mistake, considering Mummy's attempt when we lived in Stansted. It was eight years ago and I still have the scabs on my scalp as proof. I am not ashamed to be grey. I don't really care what I look like.

Auntie Trish says that your party went well. Karl had cordoned off the upstairs at Danny's Bar, and Oma had bought a chocolate cake and cooked a perspex bowl full of cocktail sausages and cold garlic bread. We took Linda's magnificent cake and fourteen candles. Auntie Trish ordered champagne and we all tried to be happy. I sat and watched as most people got drunk, listened to Oma and Trish telling me how much you would have enjoyed your party and that you and Dan were drinking champagne in heaven. Robbie and Chitson took their guitars and played 'Time of Your Life' as I cut the cake and Mummy tried to blow out the candles. We had to celebrate your birthday. I think it was the right thing to do but I feel even emptier now, a hollow man sucked dry but still standing.

There is a poem about death in which the poet describes the loss of a loved one as if he or she were a ship sailing over the horizon. The ship may be out of sight but it still exists and there are others on a distant shore waiting to welcome her into the harbour. Time is making you disappear, not from my thoughts or from my heart, but your physical presence becomes harder to recall. I walk around the house like a tiger in a cage. I have no hope of escape but I cannot accept. I punch the walls, I cry and scream silently. My mind plays tricks, going over and over that day, trying to change the sequence of events so that magically you will reappear. The next knock at the door will be you and I will take you in my arms and hug you for ever and never let you go.

Night-night, my sweet. I will come up and see you. Make sure the bugs don't bite.

Your Daddy

14 March 2006

Good morning, sweetheart,

I had to spend all day yesterday rewriting the business plan for this *Dragons' Den* thing. The first plan was really rubbish and Peter McPartland was kind enough to tell me where I had gone wrong and what I needed to do. Knowing what to do is one thing. Being able to do it is another.

Robbie was out last night with Cheese, and Horsey fell asleep at 7 p.m. He had been up until midnight the night before and the tiredness finally caught up with him. Mummy and I sat in the kitchen. The silence was overwhelming. I held Mummy's hand as she sat and stared at the pictures of you, some stuck to the big mirror on the far wall and others surrounding a candle that burns for you on the kitchen table. Quietly she began to talk and as she did so tears rolled unchecked across her cheeks. It is not the 'now' that is unbearable, it is the thought of the future, however long we have to spend without you, and as each day passes you get further away. Soon we will notice changes in Robbie and Horsey as they grow older. Already Horsey is an inch taller and Robbie shows signs of an early beard. They will turn into young men and you will remain forever frozen in time, a butterfly caught in the glass cages of our memories. This is the knowledge that brings us to our knees.

Mummy is consumed by guilt and regret. Auntie Jill is getting married to Chris Knott in September and you would have been her bridesmaid. You had never been to a wedding although you were an old hand at funerals. Mummy would have taken you to try on bridesmaids' dresses. All the things that a mother and a daughter share as they grow older together have been snatched away from you both. Mummy talked and I didn't interrupt. I can offer no comfort except to cuddle her or hold her hand. More often than not I find myself in tears, breathless and crushed by the sheer enormity of what has happened.

Mummy lives in a terrible past where she relives every cross word she ever said to you or rebukes herself for the times that she told you that you couldn't go out or that you were being too noisy or to calm down because you might upset someone. It was always left to Mummy to tell you off because I was the coward and you came to me because you knew I would be the one to say yes. Somebody said to me that daughters can wrap their fathers around their little fingers. You didn't have to wrap me around your little finger. I came ready wrapped.

Yesterday, after I had picked up Horsey from school, I drove to Sudbury to see Uncle Davy. The vans have been sign-written and he wanted me to be the first to see them. Charlie's Larder takes up at least half of one side, rendered in green and deep red and an earthy brown. Underneath your logo, Davy has added the line: 'Gourmet Foods for Chefs'. You really would love it. I do not know whether there is any kind of solace in keeping your name alive for the world to see. It is, beyond any doubt, a statement of our love for you and a reminder, perhaps to others, of the extraordinary effect you had on people in such a short time. The world was a better place when you were in it and it remains a better place because of your legacy. People think of you and smile. People think of you and do good.

The drive to Sudbury takes me on the top road past Gestingthorpe and on to Bulmer where Robbie Gladwell lives. If I look to my left I can see down and into the valley towards Belchamp church although all but the very top of the tower is hidden by trees. You are lying there next to your cousin and your grandfather but I know you are not really there and sometimes I cannot even bring myself to look in that direction. So many of your friends have been to see you. Adele and Bee went on Saturday, and Jo [Pallett] and Kevin, and on Friday Paul and Mel took Miles and left flowers for you. Mummy and I cannot go. I do not know if I ever will be able to visit you there. You are with me wherever I go and I do not have the strength to face that particular truth. Always at the back of my mind are the things that I still must do. Attend your inquest. Organise a headstone. Sign a certificate. I keep these things hidden behind a locked door in my mind and I do not know if I will ever be able to find the key.

As I drove to Sudbury you came so vividly to me. It was the last time we had visited Robbie Gladwell together. We were shocked and delighted to find that the field behind his studio ran down to the river at the back of the mill and that Belchamp church was so close that we could almost touch it. I couldn't believe that I had grown up there and spent so many hours playing in the fields and building camps, and that I had never discovered that the Bulmer road was less than a mile from the back garden of the mill. I had walked for miles in every direction but that one. How strange life is. As we waited for Robbie, you jumped up and down and pleaded with me to take you to the mill. 'It will only take a few minutes,' you said. I had told you so many stories of my childhood, growing up in what my father had called 'the forgotten valley', building camps out of straw bales in the summer and wading through flooded meadows in the winter. How Steve Butler and I had made boats out of oil drums and gone fishing for sticklebacks at the waterfall. Idyllic memories protected from the harsh truths of my parents' penury and my father's terrible illnesses. And I realised that you had never seen the mill although you had obviously re-created it in your mind from all the stories.

We set off across the field, making our way towards a line of trees guarding the small but steep bank that leads down to the stream. We held hands and ran because we didn't have much time. At the bottom of the bank, the bridge across the stream was still intact and I pointed out to you the island where Steve and I had camped when we were twelve and I had cooked raw sausages over a fire made of twigs and damp leaves. On the other side of the bridge the latch gate stood locked and we climbed over it and found ourselves in another field, knee-high grass running out under the overhang of a giant oak tree that

still stands at the bottom of the mill's garden and marks
the boundary that divides the garden from the field with
the help of a rusty barbed-wire fence. We were both
really excited. It had been many years since I had seen the
mill and you had never seen it. My mind was flooded
with childhood memories and you had asked me whether
we could buy the mill one day and I had said yes but
only if we won the Lottery because there was no other
way that we would possibly be able to afford it.

We had made it halfway across the field, the bottoms of
our trousers soaked by the damp grass, when you saw the
bull. It had been hiding under the branches of the oak
tree or waiting for us to get close enough to have
nowhere to run to. Slowly it emerged from the shadow
and stood motionless, staring at us. I told you to stop and
I could feel the excitement running through your body.
The bull made a half-step forwards and, as it did so, a
small calf appeared behind it. The bull was protecting its
child and it wouldn't charge unless we kept moving
towards it. I told you that we should turn back but slowly
without any sudden movements. Because it was you, you
argued and said that we might not ever get another
chance to see the mill and the bull would understand. I
doubted that the bull would understand and I told you
that we would have hundreds of opportunities to come
back, especially now that we had found such a fantastic
short cut.

I think that was last November, less than two weeks
before fate or something beyond our understanding took
you from us. As it happens we never did get another

opportunity to see the mill and now some part of you will be there, looking down on the house that you thought you loved for ever. I cannot write any more. I cannot hold back the tears. I love you.

My darling,

It is Wednesday morning. David Rozalla is coming
soon to help me practise for this *Dragons' Den* interview.
I have had to fill in another form which asked me for
details about my children. I cannot bear to fill in these
forms. I put all your details down and then put a note
underneath saying what happened. Mummy is still asleep.
She can no longer sleep during the night and spends hours
playing solitaire on the computer. I have been wandering
around the house, crying, helpless, knowing that the
nightmare will never end and that there will never be
another tomorrow.

I have become incredibly aware of other people's
tragedies. Day after day we are joined in purgatory by
other innocents. African children continue to die in
their thousands. Disasters strike suddenly and without
warning, extinguishing lives in less time than it takes to
blink. More than half the world knows how we feel and
yet the sense of unreality grows. Friends ring up without
mentioning you. Uncle Stu continues to apply for
absurd jobs that he has no chance of getting. His latest
idea is to become a paramedic so that he can give
something back to society. As he is a very thirsty man

with a severely disabled left foot, he may not meet all the application criteria.

I do not know what to do, what to think. Mummy said last night that she has only death to look forward to for then she might see you again, and yet she finds from somewhere the strength to laugh with Horsey and help him with his homework, and she hugs Robbie and tells him what a wonderful guitarist he is. I watch her and see how much effort she uses to maintain a veneer of normality when we are in company. There is nothing left when we are alone and then she can let go. I cuddle her partly to comfort myself because she does not come to me and what words of comfort can we offer each other? Sometimes I tell her that I know you are there, that your spirit exists and that even if we do not wholly believe, we cannot take the chance and that we must believe in you for your sake. She does not even look at me when I say this and I can feel her emptiness and despair.

We are in our cell and sometimes we sit quietly, not exactly accepting our fate but really only semi-conscious, and at other times we stand up and pound on the door, screaming and punching to be let out, but there is nobody listening and there is no key and no hope of escape. There is only one way out. We could take our own lives but we think of this only in our very darkest moments and we know that this is a coward's way out and utterly selfish.

Perhaps faith also offers hope. We walk up to Thaxted church more often now and light candles for you and sit in one of the pews, staring at the image of Christ that hangs above the altar. I cannot speak for Mummy but sometimes I try to pray although I do not know what to say or what to pray for. I pray that you are in paradise and free from pain but I do not know what that means. I do not believe in the Christian idea of heaven. I am frightened to pray for Robbie and Horsey. I prayed for you every day. I made a wish every time we passed the wishing tree and it was always the same wish. God wasn't listening then so why would he or she or whatever be listening now? Maybe God sees praying for the health and safety of an individual as selfish and punishes those who do so for their vanity and their arrogance. As I have said to you before, if God does listen to our prayers what did all the African children ever do to deserve their terrible fate?

If anything, with each passing day my sense of unreality grows. This must be a dream and soon I will wake up. It's not that I cannot live without you. I don't want to live without you.

My love will never diminish.

Daddy

Hello, my angel,

The last three days have been very busy. On
Wednesday evening Robbie played live in a pub in
Newmarket called the Palomino. I was roadie, manager
and van driver, unpaid, of course, and mostly unnoticed, I
hope, after the lights went down. The band were brilliant,
even Charlie McP's singing is getting better. I stood at the
back with a pint of shandy and thought of you and how
much you would have loved it and how proud you
would have been of Robbie. Cheese and Lou came along
as groupies and as I watched them dancing and laughing
and looking important, I could see you between them
with your arms around their shoulders, shouting for
Robbie at the top of your voice and knocking drinks out
of people's hands. I could see you so clearly, wearing your
black jeans and your black army boots with a pink hoodie,
your hair loose, a glorious chestnut-red waterfall of colour
half down your back. And then you came to sit on the
bar stool next to mine and I wanted to put my hand on
your shoulder and stroke your hair and let you take a
quick swig of my shandy when the barmaid wasn't
looking. Except you weren't really there, and Cheese and
Lou danced alone and Robbie played 'Radio' by the

Alkaline Trio just for you, and I cried in the dark where the kids couldn't see me.

On Thursday Mummy came with me to London for the screen test for *Dragons' Den*. I think I would have given you the day off school so that you could have come too. After all, it's not every day that you get to go in by the stage door at the BBC Television Centre and stand in the middle of a small white room being filmed making a complete idiot of yourself. Mummy says she is proud of me and that I did my best. You would not have been so kind. I could always rely on you to point out my failings. I kept the BBC visitors' pass as a memento of the day and when we got home I gave it to Robbie but I would have given it to you.

Paul and Mel had picked Horsey up from school and later that evening we went to get him. Paul had been out to get a takeaway and he had kept some warm for me: two vegetarian sausages and some tepid chips. I have never trusted that fish and chip shop in Elsenham. The vegetarian sausages were rock hard and utterly devoid of moisture. They retained the colour and consistency of a pair of ancient rivets rescued from a girder holding up the Humber Bridge. Still, I was grateful to Paul and the sausages were preferable to the battered sausage I bought in the Ocean Delight in Thaxted after Christmas.

I'm not much good at small talk any more. I tend to be OK for a while and then I get lost in my own thoughts. It's not so bad with Paul and Mel as they seem to understand better than most that our lives aren't normal even whilst others carry on with the same routines. I still find myself apologising for not being very interesting or falling short in the joke department. John or Stu or even Auntie Trish will ring and ask me how I am or how we are and I will say 'fine' or 'OK'. There comes a point when others don't want to know that what passes for life for us is mostly unbearable. We cannot inflict our misery on others for ever. It is hardest when I pick up Robbie from Newport, his long, pale, melancholy face partially hidden by a curtain of hair. He always asks, 'Daddy, are you all right?' I love the way he still calls me Daddy. What can I say? I must show him that I am strong and that I will never let him down even if sometimes I do. But I am not all right.

Today is your grandfather's birthday. You never knew him and he would have loved you so much. Maybe you are together now and if you are, I pray that you are looking after each other, that he has been able to find you amongst all the other souls. I remember his hands so well. He had exquisite fingers. It seems a strange word to use but I can't think of another. His fingers were long and perfectly straight, not bent and mangled like mine, and even towards the end of his life when arthritis had disfigured his knuckles, his fingers remained graceful and somehow untouched by time. He will protect you, of that I am certain.

I am no longer in the mood to recount stories or tell of the little normalities that pepper our days. I wonder again why I am writing to you. Is it to somehow keep you alive? Only when I sit here at the keyboard are we truly alone together. I walk around this house and there are

holes where you should be. The hole beside us on the
settee. The hole at the kitchen table. The hole at the top
of the stairs and the terrible quiet of your bedroom. The
hole at the school gates at half past three. The hole in the
passenger seat of the car. Everywhere I look there is a
space for you but you are not in it. I still do not
completely believe that you will not be coming back. If
the phone rings, a part of me hopes that it will be the
police to say that they have found you alive, living in a
guest house in Eastbourne, or if my mobile rings it will be
Mummy to tell me that you have come home and it was
all a dream.

We watched a film the other night called *The Constant
Gardener*. It was long and quite complicated, about the
way drug companies abuse their power, testing new
medicines on AIDS victims in Africa. In the end the hero
goes willingly to his death to be reunited with his wife of
only two years who has been murdered. As I watched the
film, I wondered how his love could be greater than
mine. How his grief could be greater than mine. But films
are not real life. He did not have two living children to
protect, a family for whom he was responsible. I am
forced by circumstance to carry on much as before, to try
to find work, to build the business, to absorb myself in the
minutiae of survival. Selling the house, going to a parents'
evening, paying the bills. But when I am alone in bed or
lying on the floor, staring unseeing into the dark, I
wonder about the man that I would wish to be. A father
that you would be proud of. A selfless man who might
make a difference for his own sake and for the sake of his

daughter. I hope I have the courage to be something better than I am and to carry your undying light with me into the unknown.

It is half past two in the morning. Mummy is still awake doing the crossword in the kitchen. I have just heard the milkman noisily leaving tomorrow's milk on the porch. I am going to try to sleep now and dream of you.

I love you.

Daddy

Hello, my darling angel,

It is Monday morning. The weekend has disappeared, eaten up with endless journeys to and from Newport, to Cambridge with Robbie and Cheese to take them to a party that turned out to be a disaster and to Audley End to pick up Toby who came to see us yesterday but without Laura.

I had a terrible headache for most of Saturday and looking back, I think it was because I had forgotten to take my pills for a couple of days. I have felt for some time that they are making no difference but now I am not so sure. On Friday I felt as if I was shaking myself to pieces, like an old car without suspension, bumping and cursing its way along a raggedy road. Every little thing was too much to bear. A raised voice, the cat's miaow. I kept knocking things over and bursting into tears. I am frightened to think that I might be dependent but I remembered the pill again on Sunday and today I feel calmer.

Toby stayed for Sunday lunch which we had at the usual time at around 6 p.m. We talked about Network Rail and the lawyers. It must be two weeks since the letter of claim was sent but we have heard nothing.

Similarly I have heard nothing from Tony Blair but that is to be expected. The police rang over the weekend to say that there is to be a public inquiry and that the rail company would like to meet us beforehand. I have no intention of meeting with them. They have not had the common decency to write to us or offer any kind of support or condolence. Their behaviour, has, in my opinion, been less than human.

The Reverend Titford is coming in an hour. I have told you about him before. He took your service at Belchamp and he has remained in regular contact. At first his silence and unforced gentility was unnerving but I have grown to be very fond of him and his visits provide some comfort, an opportunity to be ourselves without masks or forced laughter. I have kept Robbie and Horsey at home so that they can see him too. Robbie is stumbling through each day, raging at the world and furious with God. I have noticed with Horsey that his outer skin is very thin. He seems the most controlled and capable of all of us but if I so much as raise my voice to him, he cannot cope and retreats in tears, curling up in a ball in the corner of the room. Mummy and I give all that we can, hugging them, soothing them, trying to give them confidence, but I do not know and can only guess at what goes on in their heads. They must be so frightened, so angry. They should be looking forward to their lives without fear and yet they have both seen at first-hand the frailty of existence.

Because it was Sunday again yesterday, I have been reading the papers. I can't help myself. I make a cup of tea, I roll a cigarette, I sit at the kitchen table with my photographs of you and flick through the colour supplements. I read an article about an actor called Paul Bettany who has survived terrible personal tragedy to become a movie star. You saw him in *Master and Commander* with Russell Crowe, a film you liked very much. His brother died at the age of eight in an accident at school when Paul Bettany was sixteen. He went off the rails, left school, hung around in London, got into drugs. Robbie is sixteen. I feel that if I make one wrong move, I could lose him. We are walking across ice so thin that with each step it cracks beneath our feet and there is no safe ground in sight. In the article the actor says that his parents divorced under the strain and that his father came close to suicide, finally deciding that he was bisexual and going to live with a man in a cottage in Scotland. Is this what lies in store for me?

My sweetheart,

I am sorry I didn't finish writing to you yesterday. A
succession of people came to the door and then I had to go
to Sudbury where the embers of the day suddenly exploded,
a forgotten firework in the ashes. Before the Reverend
Titford arrived, Mags turned up unexpectedly. Remember I
told you that her house burnt down and she is living with
Jim. I went to see her last week and when she returned the
compliment, she told me the same story again, almost word
for word. I like her very much though. She is kind and
thoughtful and has endured much. She did tell me that she
had bought a Dyson vacuum cleaner to clean Jim's house
and discovered that the carpets are pink and not brown. It
was news to Jim too.

Mags left to make way for the Reverend and he stayed
for two hours. We sat in the kitchen and drank tea and
ate chocolate biscuits. Mummy joined us and he spoke
again of your 'Charlieness' as he calls it and his certainty
that the essence of you cannot be extinguished. I told him
that we go to church more often but that I am unable to
pray in any traditional sense. For my part I just sit facing
the altar, surrounded by peacefulness and what he calls the
link with eternity that the church provides. It is a beautiful

idea and there is a permanence about the church, a sense of generations past and generations yet to come. Mummy said that she finds some comfort in the kindness of our friends and in the little things that they do: flowers left on the doorstep, a card on your birthday, a simple phone call. In the post this morning we received a letter from the Reverend containing a page photocopied from a book with a section underlined. I do not know the source but this is what it says:

'The sudden, inexplicable kindness of strangers is the best thing in the universe and it is uniquely human.'

Later on I went to Sudbury because Oma rang and said that she was ill and needed some tablets for vomiting and diarrhoea, as she succinctly put it. Poor Oma, she sounded terrible. I went straight to her, calling Uncle Davy on the way in the hope that he might be able to spare five minutes between visits to the cash and carry and whichever meetings were set to crowd out his day. I missed him because he had gone to Belchamp to see you and Dan and Daddy, our own unique corner of the graveyard. For a moment I thought that I might go with him but I am not ready.

I was surprised to find Oma up and although there were dark circles under her eyes, she looked alive and pleased to see me. By this time my daily headache had moved up several gears, a small herd of thundering buffalo ceaselessly searching for a way out of my head. She offered me tea, which I made for myself, and we sat in her kitchen and talked about Uncle Davy and Auntie Franky, both of us unaware of the storm to come.

She had bought us some Aberdeen steak mince and some individual apple pies with pre war packaging that must have come from ALDI.

I was about to leave when we somehow got on to the subject of teaching or, more specifically, the subject of my becoming a teacher. I understand Oma. She is my mother and she cares for me just as I care for you and Robbie and Horsey. I know that her heart is broken for us and that she only wants us to be safe and secure but she is a human battering ram, wholly inflexible and absolutely sure that her way is the right way and, very probably, the only way. Sometimes I cannot cope with her sheer intensity. My track record over the last few years is pretty crap, I admit, and I have always been honest about that. In order to avoid an argument I retreated like a man trying to pedal backwards up a cliff but hampered by the buffalo in my head and what I suppose must be self-pity, my temper snapped and I fought back. At one point Oma said that I must be a nightmare to live with and I am sure she is right. I wouldn't want to live with me. Eventually the argument reached a kind of furious crescendo and Oma told me to 'get out and never come back'. All I had done was not agree with her. I had shouted and at one point, I accidentally punched myself in the groin in frustration. I had been aiming for my leg but missed. My headache was so bad that I thought I was going to pass out and some invisible man was wrapping barbed wire around my chest. The storm passed as storms do and I left her on kind of speaking terms, a mumbled apology from us both.

My darling,

Once again I failed to find the time to return to the keyboard and so it is Wednesday morning. The sun is shining between flotillas of white fluffy clouds moving like giant turtles across the sky. There are few signs of spring except for the occasional battalion of tired-looking snowdrops. It remains very cold and I have yet to see a single daffodil.

I have made my peace with Oma and I may go to see her this afternoon. I received an e-mail from Saffron Walden County High School in which they have asked me to go in after Easter and teach the sixth form film studies on a voluntary basis. No money as usual but great experience if I do decide to try to become a proper teacher. Oma is very pleased. It will bring her some peace and maybe a little happiness if I can find a vocation before she dies.

Last night Mummy and I went to Horsey's parents' evening. It was the first time that Mummy has been back to the school since we went to your parents' evening in November. The hall was packed with parents and children and all your old teachers. I had my arm around Mummy's waist and she put her head on my shoulder, her hair

sliding across her face, disguising a single tear. We queued
up first to see Miss Kelly, the Italian teacher who had said
such wonderful things about you. How you had a real
flair for languages and a wonderful 'ear' and how she so
looked forward to teaching you in the years to come. She
said much the same about Horsey who sat stone-faced
between us, but, like you, the words come easily to him
and he has a fantastic memory. Miss Luckes, the
geography teacher, had tears in her eyes. She took
Mummy's hand in hers and told her that she would look
after Horsey and that if there was anything that she could
do for us, we had only to ask. We had never met her
before because she didn't teach you, a lovely young
woman in a natty grey suit. We went to see Mr Wyckes,
your head of year, who stood to shake our hands and he
too had tears in his eyes. He spoke at your service and
said that it had been an honour and one of the hardest
things that he has ever had to do. Sean Geraghty's mother,
Rita, took Mummy in her arms, crying so hard that her
cheeks were smudged with black make-up. It was an
ordeal, more for Mummy than for me because I have to
go to the school every day and I have built up some
defences. I went outside at one point to make a phone
call and standing by the doors, I looked around and you
were there, leaning against the brick just as you had been
the last time, after one of Mr Partridge's interminable
music evenings when you had to go out because you
couldn't take it any more. I could see you just as you
were, wearing Mummy's blue jeans, your hair loose about
your shoulders, a tiny T-shirt revealing your midriff and a

look of defiance on your face. You had your left leg raised and your foot flat against the wall to support yourself. You must have been so cold but you said that you weren't although I could clearly see you shivering. I worried so much that you would be ill. I worried about you getting a cold. I didn't worry about you going to Cambridge and catching the train. I didn't worry about that. It never occurred to me.

We received a parcel in the post this morning from the Falkland Islands, from Liam's parents. I couldn't imagine what it would be and when I opened it I found a certificate saying that they had adopted a King penguin and named it after you. There was a magnificent photograph of Charlie the penguin, standing alone on a rock overlooking a raging sea. I am going to have it framed and hang it where everyone can see it, wherever we live. There was a letter from Andrea, Liam's mother, saying that they think of us every day and that they pray for you.

Auntie Franky sends me messages from Rome saying that she sees your face in the cherry blossom or peering from behind the clouds and that you are dancing on the wind. From America we get news that Mummy's cousins in Minnesota are praying for you at their special church.

The Reverend Titford told us that the word 'religion' comes from the Latin word *religio* meaning to reconnect and that the true purpose of religion is to bring people together, to help them to 'connect' with each other and with the guiding spirit, whoever or whatever that may be. If that is true, then you are helping people to reconnect from all around the world. Even though I cannot see you, I think that I know that you are there. Your life force is so strong. Already you have changed people's lives. John Keeling rang me this morning to say that his ex-wife called him and suggested that they go on holiday as a family, taking their two daughters to Majorca in May. John said that when he told Amber and Seren, their faces lit up and he could not remember seeing them happier.

Hello, angel,

Once again the day disappeared before I had time to finish. It ended up a day in hell although every day is a day in hell.

I let Robbie stay in Newport after school and when I returned home with Horsey, I made the mistake of sorting through the unpaid bills and trying to organise my desk. We received a county court judgment from Powergen because they said we had not paid a bill for £359. I wouldn't mind except the bill wasn't for us. We have mistakenly being paying the bills for number 11 Park Street as well as our own. I rang the helpline, which is obviously of no help whatsoever, and spent nearly an hour trying to persuade a gentleman with hearing disabilities that number 11 Park Street and The Maltings are two different places, very possibly in two different towns.

'Well, somebody's been using this electricity,' he said, 'and somebody is going to have to pay for it.'

'Fine,' I said. 'You're somebody. You pay for it.'

If bailiffs come to the door they will find it has been a wasted trip. Finally I finished not paying the bills.

It was around six o'clock when Paul and Mel arrived with two bottles of wine. I rang Robbie at 7 p.m. He sounded absolutely desolate, his voice low and bleak and hopeless. I said that I would come and pick him up from Newport straightaway but he didn't want me to. He was in tears when the call ended and I didn't know what to do, whether to go and get him or wait until later as he had asked. I decided to go later but I couldn't concentrate and although Paul and I embarked upon one of our more absurd conversations concerning home-made go-karts and the perils of skateboarding down very steep hills, my mind was elsewhere. All the time Mummy and Mel were drinking more and more wine. Mel is amazing. I don't think that I have ever seen her drunk but Mummy becomes morose and the drink depresses her although she would argue that she couldn't be more depressed.

I went to get Robbie after ten and when we got back, both Paul and Mel were comforting Mummy who was bereft, crying softly, which to me is so much more desperate than Uncle Davy's terrible wailing. Robbie hadn't said a word in the car and he went straight to his room, slamming the door and, from the sound of it, knocking over huge piles of bricks with extreme force. Paul and Mel, always sensitive, discreetly took their leave but not before I had failed to persuade Mummy not to go upstairs to see Robbie. A thick silence descended on the kitchen. Horsey, mercifully spared, was immersed in a wholly inappropriate episode of *South Park* in the living room. After a while I went to stand on the stairs to see whether I could hear what was going on. Within seconds Robbie appeared, the knuckles of his left hand covered in blood from where he had punched the wall. 'I don't want you listening to me when I'm on the phone,' he screamed, pushing past me and disappearing out of the front door in only his socks. I could hear Mummy crying in the upstairs bathroom.

Eventually Mummy came down of her own accord. I tried to coax her but Mummy will only come when she wants to. I found Robbie sitting on the doorstep freezing, the cold had calmed him down and he came in quietly, even hugging me as he did so. I checked on Horsey who was asleep on the settee and then I found Mummy in her usual chair in the kitchen. She was still crying but there were no words. I knelt on the floor in front of her and put my arms around her waist and buried my head in her sweater. I felt her rest her arm across my shoulders but nothing would stop her tears. Soon I was crying too and we seemed to cry together for so long. It was as if the dam had finally broken and the grief just kept on coming out, water from an endless lake, and if we cried all night it would make no difference. If we cry for ever it will make no difference.

They are all asleep now. I don't know what time it is. Somehow I must get Robbie and Horsey up to go to school tomorrow. Something changed tonight. I think Mummy has fallen further. As you get further away, she finds being without you harder and harder to bear. For myself, the sense of unreality is only broken when I wake up briefly from the nightmare to find that the dream is real. I think of you all the time and when I find myself not thinking of you, I bring an image of you to mind and listen to your voice in my head. But for the last few days I haven't been able to hear you with the same clarity and when I look for you, I can see you only through mist as if I am looking through a frosted-glass window. I was standing behind you in the queue and suddenly a fat man has pushed in between us. I say I cannot bear to be without you and I am not sure what that means. I have to bear it. I have to try to find work. I have to look after Robbie and Horsey and Mummy. I have to go to sleep and get up in the morning but the cold horror of your absence is eating my spirit. What is important is that Robbie and Horsey are given the chance to have a good life, to see the beauty in the world and to experience love and joy as well as sadness.

I love you more than any words can ever say.

Night-night.

Your Daddy

Hello, my sweetheart,

It is midnight on Sunday, Mother's Day. Friday and Saturday came and went. On Friday I had to do some deliveries for Uncle Davy, the Whitehall Hotel in Broxted which is staffed by strange, very tense French people, and a new account near Southend. I had to pass close to the *QE2* bridge and the sight of it opened a whole new casket of memories. We would travel over the *QE2* bridge only if we were going on holiday, on our way to Dover to catch the ferry to France and then the long drive south. From the very top of the bridge you could see London and if you looked down you could see cargo ships at Tilbury docks, small enough to fold up and stow with the luggage in the back of the car.

Last year was our first without a holiday, the first time we had failed to find even enough money to go camping for a week in some rain-drenched corner of northern France. The bridge was the gateway and I stared at its majestic arch, made more so by the industrial desolation lying in its wake. So many memories. Even before Horsey was born we went to a small seaside town in Normandy called Raguenes. We must have been well off at the time because we took a mobile home rather than a tent. I can

see you standing in what passed for its dining room,
wearing a blue, velvety dress and those white, corduroy
tights that I haven't thought of in years. You were
eighteen months old.

The other thing I remember from that holiday was the
case of your mysterious nosebleed and spending two hours
in a rural French doctor's surgery with you screaming on
my lap. The French doctor, who may have been a man
but was probably a woman, eventually removed a long
and razor-sharp blade of grass from your left nostril. How
did you do it? What was the grass doing up your nose in
the first place? I wonder if I will ever be able to recall the
sound of your voice when you were that age or the
words you must have said, if time will help me remember,
opening up the locked doors in my mind.

I remember Pont l'Évêque where we camped in the
grounds of a beautiful chateau and in the mornings we
would leave Mummy and Robbie and Horsey asleep and
go to feed the horses grazing in a paddock behind the
castle. That was the holiday where Horsey fell backwards
off a swing and split his head open, and it was also where
we heard from a French lady in the supermarket that
Princess Diana had died and none of us could believe it.

Most vivid at the moment are the holidays in the south
near Montpellier and Béziers, pictures of you wrapped in a
towel on the beach at Agde, your hair straggling across
your shoulders, matted by the sun and the sea, your face
red and beaming. You urging me to hire one of those
ghastly pedalo things, or to take you for a ride on a giant
inflatable sausage, or maybe just lying down next to

Mummy and sunbathing while Robbie and Horsey and I built sandcastles or played skimming stones in the surf. Sometimes Robbie and Horsey would bury you in sand while you were snoozing and stand triumphantly on top of you only to be hurled off as you rose like an angry crab from your lair.

I suppose that I must be lucky to have such memories because maybe that's all life is, a collection of memories. And maybe you were lucky too, to have done so much. I can see you holding Sean the alligator with its bandaged snout at Gatorland when we went to Florida, and at Seaworld where they picked you out of the crowd to dance with the dolphins. I can hear you laughing next to me as we sat in the front row at the Shamu show and the killer whale fixed us with its huge but beady eye and then, with one enormous flick of its tail, drowned us in forty gallons of freezing sea water. And it was always, 'Again, Daddy, again' because the days were never long enough and there were always too many exciting things to do. At least you were happy, that's what Robbie said.

I do not want to go on holiday again.

Mrs Wiggett called this morning to ask after Mummy. She is a loyal and wonderful friend and I am grateful for her relentless good humour but sometimes I am not up to the banter. Even a short call from Mrs Wiggett is like going on stage. Sometimes I forget my lines or I am simply not in the mood. Normally when people ring and ask me how I am, I say that I am OK. I don't say I'm fine because I'm not fine and to say I'm fine would be a pretence too far. My voice must have betrayed me to Mrs

Wiggett because she asked me what the matter was. What did she think had happened? That I had stubbed my toe or accidentally burnt the breakfast or that the cat had crapped in the bedroom? It's not her fault. How can anyone understand except those others unlucky enough to suffer as we do.

It's nearly four months now.

I bought Mummy three small bunches of flowers from the Spar. One from you and one each from Robbie and Horsey. Mummy woke up at twelve and I gave her the flowers and a cup of tea. There was no point in cooking her breakfast because she wouldn't have eaten it. I told her that the flowers were from you and her face, already crumpled by sleep, seemed to collapse. She made her way to the kitchen and I could hear her singing under her breath, almost chanting, repeating over and over again, 'Whatcha doin'?' It's what you would always say to Mummy whenever you found her busy, cooking or ironing or wrapping presents or helping Horsey with his homework.

You loved Mother's Day. Last year you did everything for Mummy. You made her a fantastic card and then cooked her breakfast, followed by an extraordinary lunch. I'm sure it was a kind of hotpot of as many different kinds of vegetables as you could think of, cooked in garlic and herbs with rice and warm bread. I remember it being delicious because you saved some for me although I may have had to spend some considerable time on the lavatory as a result. Watching you cook was like being in the audience at *The Muppet Show*. Even to make the simplest thing, you would use every single pan and all the cutlery. After no time at all you would be ankle-deep in flour, potato peelings, salt and discarded herbs and you wouldn't tolerate any interference. You cooked as you did everything else, with a kind of joyful abandon.

Later in the day Auntie Pat and Mummy's cousin Richard came to see us. We had known they were coming and Mummy made old-fashioned sandwiches, you know the kind, white bread with the crusts cut off with ham and cheese and no pickle, just the way old people like them. Auntie Pat is Grandy's sister. She must be at least eighty-five and she walks with a stick, but her eyes were sparkling and her cheeks still held the flush of not quite forgotten youth. You met her several times. Once about eight years ago when we all went to a fireworks party at Cousin Gerard's house in London. I remember standing with you and Robbie on the balcony outside Gerard's bedroom and later sitting with you on my lap, talking to Uncle Ted who told us stories about the war and his fear of polished wooden floors. Uncle Ted is still alive but he is in a nursing home. His mind still works but his body is giving up.

After Pat and Richard left, Mummy cooked a roast and we ate together in the living room and watched *24*.

I do not know how to comfort Mummy. She has been crying for much of the day although she showed tremendous courage with Pat. I circle my arms around her to try to hug her, hoping that my physical presence will provide some kind of protection, to show her that I love her but she doesn't respond. I sense that she is waiting for me to stop. I feel almost as if I am interrupting her and that she is with you in some way that I can't understand.

I am too tired now. It is 1.30 a.m. There is school in the morning and only a week until the Easter holidays.

You know I love you.

Night-night, my darling.

Daddy

Hello, my Charlikins,

We have survived two more days. This morning I had a meeting at Saffron Walden County High School and as a result I will be the guest lecturer in Film and Media studies after the Easter holidays. I have some old A-level papers to help me prepare and I must submit the guidelines for my lectures by 19 April. If I do well they may ask me to do some more and I may yet end up a teacher, albeit an old one with thoughts of early retirement.

I have heard nothing from *Dragons' Den*. If we do not hear by Friday, then we have failed to clear the final hurdle. I won't be too despondent. If it happens, it happens.

I saw Oma again on Monday. We haven't argued for several days although there is no let-up in the intensity of our conversations. Oma knows that I have been writing to you and recently she asked whether she could read what I have written so far. At first I refused saying that I would let her read the finished thing but not the work in progress. And then I thought that I might never finish or if I do, it will only be because a day will come when it won't feel right any more or I will find some other way to talk to you and what does it matter anyway? This is not some work of fiction to be edited and criticised. So I let Oma read what I have written. I hope you don't mind. She loves you so much.

So it was on Monday that I went to retrieve the manuscript, all 150 pages of it. She had read it all over the weekend and she handed it back to me in its green folder, her hands trembling. It was, she said, an extraordinary experience and although she had spent much of the time crying, she had been disturbed by the depths of our misery. She had not realised just how devastated we are, how completely our lives have been overturned. I looked at her when she said this, not unkindly, and for once I managed to think before responding.

'Why would we not be devastated?' I said. 'What else have we but misery and regret?'

I cannot remember her exact words but she said something like – 'You have a life to live, a duty to your sons, a duty to you. What's done is done and cannot be undone.'

And as we talked I understood why she is like she is and why our generation is so unprepared to cope with death and catastrophe. As you know she grew up in the war, in an industrial city in Holland that was occupied by the Nazis. She lived with death on a daily basis. She learnt to expect it. Once, when she was only seventeen, she was taken at gunpoint by the Gestapo, the German secret police, and interrogated about her friendship with a Jewess who was later arrested and taken to Auschwitz. She told me that she would walk down the street behind her father and mother and imagine that she was following their coffins. She lost friends and relations, blown to bits by German bombs, and death was commonplace.

Perhaps she is right. We have become soft, selfish and weak. As a society we are obsessed with ourselves, with money, power, appearance, status, all things that are superficial and ultimately meaningless. But knowledge of our weakness, our self-loathing, does not make your loss any easier to bear. For all Oma's experience, for all the horror that she has witnessed, she has never lost a child. We do try, we do go on, there is still occasional laughter, but your absence accompanies us everywhere and we cannot let you go.

Oma made another observation. That I idolise you. That you could be very naughty, as if somehow I have not reminded you of all the bad things you did. I don't remember you doing any bad things. You could be naughty. In fact, at times, you were probably the naughtiest child I have ever come across, but you were never mean and you were never malicious. You never sought to embarrass or torment anybody less fortunate than yourself. Of course there were occasions when you went out of your way to make my life a misery but, looking back, most of the time I deserved it. There were also times when I made your life a misery and I would do anything now to take back some of the cruel things I said to you. The times that I made you cry because you had made me so angry that I would go almost cross-eyed with rage. You were normal and I loved you so much and I love you so much. I am lost without you.

Every night Mummy repeats to herself what you used to say when you went to bed: 'Night–night, sleep well. Come up and see me.'

On Saturday it will be four months.

Goodnight, my darling,

Daddy

Sweetheart,

It is Friday afternoon. The school has broken up for the Easter holidays. Horsey has gone to stay with Jonny and Robbie is in his room. He wants me to take him to Newport later so Mummy and I will be alone again. We may go over to see the Wiggetts but Mummy is sleeping on the settee and she may not wake up in time. Paul and Mel are going out but we will probably see them tomorrow.

It has been a beautiful day, a fresh wind full of the promise of spring and it is almost warm enough to wear a T-shirt. There are daffodils out, a small bunch up by the pond in the corner of the garden, and there are buds on some of the trees. There is something basic inside me that wants to celebrate. Had you been here I would have been gardening all afternoon, clearing away the dregs of winter, mowing the lawn, removing dead weeds and leaves from the flower beds. I might even have cut back the ivy from the corner of the wall by the road but I can't. I can't do anything. I feel an overwhelming sense of guilt and regret. I feel guilty if an hour goes by in which I don't think of you. I feel guilty if I laugh. I feel guilty if I watch a film or read a book that gives me pleasure. If only I had the certainty of faith.

During the last two days, the mist has cleared and memories of you have circled my mind like hungry seagulls, screeching and swooping and endlessly chattering. Snatches of conversation pass through me like train carriages hurrying through the night. I can remember what it was like to be happy. On a day like today, lying on our backs holding hands on the trampoline in the garden at Debden Green, staring up into a cloudless sky, listening to the querulous chatter of the starlings hiding somewhere in the roof. Of course there were bad times, arguments, evenings wasted spent alone in your room, misunderstandings and disappointments. But these moments passed and the clear blue sky of contentment always returned.

I am fairly sure that I will be able to go on although I have no idea how I will feel in six months' time. I cannot predict how I will feel tomorrow. I think I will be able to work, to go through the motions of life, and I will do my best to look after Robbie and Horsey. I will look after Mummy too if she will let me. I cannot imagine looking forward to anything again. And I feel guilty for saying that. A constant struggle goes on inside my head, arguments and counter-arguments go back and forth like a ping-pong ball. How do I reconcile your loss with making the most of the life I have left? I can't bear it when people say to me that you would want us to be happy.

I know what the answer is. Life has to have a purpose. Revenge isn't a purpose, not for me anyway. We have heard nothing from the lawyers, which means that they have not heard from Network Rail. Eventually we will hear, of course. They will deny negligence and we will not have the money to fight them. We will try to keep the fight going by raising support locally, picketing the station, asking people to sign a petition and maybe we will get some press coverage. I know that we must fight to make the station safer, it is the least that we must do. But after that, what then? I can't just go on living the same life.

I talk to Mummy and tell her that we must devote our lives to others, go to Africa, do something to help even one other person to have a better life or to live rather than die. But we can't do it yet because we have to guide Robbie and Horsey through school and we must always be there for them. The answer is that I don't know what to do. In films and books it is always so straightforward. In real life people don't run away to live in a hut in the mountains or sell everything up to while away their years on a Greek island. I'm not going to join a monastery, at least I don't think I am. I'm not going to become a paragliding instructor or a faith healer or row single-handed across the Atlantic. Or maybe I will do all of these things in a future I can't see or understand or bear to think about.

Adele came yesterday. She told Mummy that Becka had called from Africa and asked what your favourite flower was. Adele didn't know and neither, for that matter, do I. Anyway Becka said that it should have been an iris because Iris was the name of the goddess of rainbows and you were like a rainbow. And then the most amazing thing happened. Adele looked out of the window as she was talking and a perfect, dazzling rainbow spanned the sky. I saw the light come into Mummy's eyes and for a moment a smile creased the corners of her mouth.

Perhaps you brought the rainbow, my sweetheart. I want to believe that more than I want to believe anything. The past seems so long ago. I would give my life just to see you again.

Mummy is awake and we are going to the Wiggetts'. Alan is cooking meatballs and pasta just like his mother used to make.

I will write again soon.

I love you.

Your Daddy

Hello, poppet,

Another Sunday. The beginning of our fifth month without you. Yesterday was not a good day.

I had another row with Oma. She rang in the morning and even on the phone, I could hear her moving her siege engines into place, preparing to bombard me with ideas, observations, reasons for the hideous situation in which we find ourselves. Just once, I'd like to share a conversation with her about the weather or politics or gardening or some gossip about the woman next door. The doctor has put her on some pills called beta blockers. They are for anxiety and high blood pressure. Oma is very worried about them and the possible side effects. I pray for her sake that they work. She lies awake all night, every night, worrying about us and then she transfers that worry to my shoulders. Sometimes the burden is too great. She takes her microscope to every aspect of our lives, unable to bear the way we live, the fact that there are piles of ironing in the bedroom, too many toys on Horsey's bedroom shelves, that there is a mountain of paperwork on my desk, that we shop in Tesco instead of ALDI, that we have a car we can't afford. She wants to buy me new clothes because I am too scruffy and she is frightened that

I may get an interview for a job and my prospective employers may run screaming from the interview room upon seeing me, the unshaven bagman from Thaxted. I am forty-eight years old. I am past the point where I am going to allow my mother to buy me clothes, especially clothes of her choice.

I rang Oma back in the afternoon. I cannot accept the conflict. On some things Oma and I will never agree but she is my mother and I understand more than ever her love for me and the depths of her worry. Sometimes I think it would be nice for the children to have a cosy grandmother who sits knitting by the fire and tells stories of sepia-etched days when the world was young, but our life has not allowed Oma the freedom or the peace to be a figure from a fairytale and it is up to me to control my temper.

The rest of Saturday drifted by. We watched television in the evening and Robbie went to stay with Will Holt for the night. I can't say I wasn't worried. Will spends his life as if he has just been launched from a catapult but I must trust Robbie and he rang early this morning to say that he was all right.

Spring has definitely arrived. The sun shines between perpetual showers and the grass has suddenly woken up and appears to grow before our very eyes. I stood in the kitchen staring out of the window, trying to find the energy and the desire needed to get out the lawnmower. Eventually I just did it and afterwards I raked the flower beds and threw the slaughtered mice on to a pile behind the bamboo that grows next to the garage. Had you been here I would have celebrated with a beer and nagged Mummy to come out to admire my handiwork but there is no longer any pleasure in these small achievements.

I have been to Newport to get Robbie and Cheese. Mummy is cooking a roast and later, as has become our routine, we will watch *24* and go to bed. Mummy has given up sleeping through the night and now she plays cards until the early hours and compensates for her lack of sleep during the day. I am going to see Dr Tayler in the morning.

Bless you my angel.

Sleep well.

Daddy

Hello again, poppet,

Spring has definitely sprung as they say. I have discarded my winter sweater and in a minute I am going to brave the walk up to the Spar in my T-shirt to buy a paper and some dishwasher tablets.

I saw Dr Tayler yesterday at the surgery. He was, as always, deeply concerned and although the waiting room was very busy, he spared me more than half an hour. We have been on the pills for at least two months and I told him that neither Mummy nor I can tell whether they have any effect or not. We are on the lowest dosage but any more and he fears that we may be turned into zombies and perhaps it is better to feel the pain than spend our days staring blankly into space. He asked whether we wanted to go back to see the psychiatrist but I declined, not knowing what a psychiatrist or anybody else can say to make things any better.

You come in waves now, images of you standing by the door, one hand on your hip, looking bored, waiting for me to find my wallet or my phone or both before we can go out. I see you crouching in the garden stroking the cat or walking across the road on your way back from school. Often I imagine you walking down the stairs, the heaviness of your footfall making the whole house shake. More often now I go into your room or stand in the doorway. Mummy has tidied your clothes up from the floor and made your bed but apart from that everything remains the same. I see you lying asleep, curled up like a cashew nut, sucking your thumb. I can count your freckles and I know the perfect texture of your skin. Your startling copper-gold hair is fanned out across your pillow and I know every curl and kink. When you were younger you used to talk gibberish in your sleep and Mummy and I would creep into your bedroom and listen to you in wonder. What dreams you must have had. Sometimes you would shout, catching us by surprise – 'No, no, get out' – or 'Put it down, Robbie'. You never seemed frightened, angry sometimes, but never frightened. It was as if you lived as passionately in your dreams as when you were awake. Life was made for you. When you ate an apple, you would eat everything, the core, the skin, the pips. I bought you mangoes in the supermarket, which you would eat in the car on the way home, gnawing the flesh from the giant stone in the middle. How can life be taken away from someone who loved it so much? I will never be able to answer this question.

The police called again this morning. A man from the RAIB (Rail Accident Investigation Bureau) wants to come and see us next week. The police say it will be a private meeting and anything we say will be treated with complete confidentiality. I don't want what we say to be confidential. I want these bastards to make the station safer. We still haven't heard from Network Rail. We still don't know when your inquest will take place. We heard from Tony Blair's press secretary. Apparently the Prime Minister is too busy to reply to every letter he receives. Too busy to care about one beautiful schoolgirl, obliterated in the blink of an eye for being in the wrong place at the wrong time. I wonder how these people would feel if they had lost their child. Whether they would be too busy then.

Tonight I have promised to take Horsey to the cinema to see a movie called *The Ringer* and tomorrow we are going to Whizz Kids in Cambridge for Horsey's second audition. He has been practising, doing the most alarming dance in which all his limbs go in different directions at once. Mummy and I take cover behind the settee in case his arms fly off. I have asked Robbie and Cheese to come with us this evening so that we can try to be a family but Cheese and her mother seem to be rowing all the time and I am worried that we are coming between them. Cheese spends so much time here and I am sure that her mother misses her. I am trying to encourage her to spend more time at home without upsetting her or Robbie. It is a task that requires the most delicate touch, something I am not renowned for.

I can only say that I love you. I feel you slipping away and I don't know how to cope with it. I am walking along the edge of a cliff but there is an invisible barrier between me and the precipice. Sometimes I want to throw myself off but I know that I can't. Mummy was right. Our lives did end when we lost you and now we are starting a new life, stripped of hope and happiness but still important. It is as if I have been watching you fall from a great height and you have been getting smaller and smaller and now I can't see you but I know you are there although I know you will never come back. I could jump after you but I might not find you.

I try to keep you with me all the time, dipping into memories, like a kid at a tombola stall. Sometimes I keep getting the same one. When I came to pick you up from Brighton in the summer. I had wanted to leave almost straightaway but it was only about 6.00 p.m. and you persuaded me that we all still had time to go down to the pier. The rain had stopped in preparation for our departure and a timid sun peered from around the clouds. I parked on the front and we walked along the beach and then made our way up several flights of steps to the pier's entrance. You and I were miles ahead of Horsey and Mummy who walk as if time has no meaning, so slowly that they are almost in reverse. You, shouting at them to get a move on, and eventually we got bored with waiting and ran down the length of the pier to the rollercoasters at the end. I bought you £10 worth of tickets and two hot dogs, one for me and one for you, and prepared to sit on a bench and watch you. You mooched around, unimpressed by what you saw.

As you were a veteran of Alton Towers, Thorpe Park and even Bush Gardens, only the highest, fastest and scariest rides were good enough for you. You turned your nose up at the rollercoaster and eventually you settled on the Waltzer, what I used to call the Skid when I was young, as the only ride remotely hideous enough to satisfy you. But you wouldn't get on without me and by this time Horsey and Mummy had disappeared into the Doctor Who exhibition, much to your disgust.

At first I refused. The last time I went on the Skid, I threatened to kill the operator unless he stopped it and let me get off. Then I had to lie down for an hour before I could walk. But you wouldn't give up and I thought that maybe, just maybe, I would be able to bear it. So we got on together and I asked you to hold my hand which you did because there was nobody else on the ride. I lasted about one and half spins before I had to wave my arms about frantically to get it to stop. I crawled off and lay in a ball by the hotdog stand while you insulted me and told me how pathetic I was.

Robbie and Horsey hate theme parks. They have both inherited my stomach. They can only put up with things that go in a straight line. So I will probably never go to a theme park again. Never see your face a mask of pure joy.

I am trying to think of your life as a whole, not as a life cut short. Trying to convince myself that you packed so much in that you just used up your time more quickly than the rest of us. It doesn't really work.

Mummy is eating more, not much more but more. She hasn't lost any more weight but she is still terribly thin. She has to stoop or her jeans fall off when she walks.

Hello, my Charlikins,

I have been becalmed for the last three days, lost in thought and drifting on bleak seas.

David Rozalla, a knight in shining armour, has come to our rescue again. He has set up a company to republish your grandfather's books on-line and he has agreed to pay me to do all the scanning and initial editing. I have been busy collating material and talking to Oma about my father's early life so that I can write a dedicated home page. Robbie has been helping me figure out which buttons do what on the scanner which David Rozalla has also paid for. I owe debts of gratitude to many people and I hope, one day, to be able to pay them all back.

We are also lucky to have a wonderful bank manager. Her name is Faye and not only has she agreed to cover our mortgage payments until the house is sold, but when she heard what had happened, she sent a most beautiful bouquet of flowers. They say that you reap what you sow in life but it isn't true. You, above all, deserved a long and happy life filled with adventure and laughter.

I met Joan walking up to the post office yesterday. She is the old lady who lives in one of the cottages behind our house. I didn't know that you used to call in on her almost every day to check whether she was all right and to see whether she needed anything. We stood talking together outside the Thaxted Tyre Company for about ten minutes. She said that she will never forget you and that she prays for you every day. Tears came into her eyes and I didn't know what to say to her. 'God takes the best ones,' she said. 'He always has.'

Horsey passed the second audition for Whizz Kids. The third audition is next Tuesday. If he passes that, they will offer him a place starting in September. He's really excited and keeps offering to look after us when we are old. He has been practising his Oscar acceptance speech, which seems to include a proud mention for everybody except me. I don't mind. Mummy is the power behind the throne.

It's late now. Robbie has come back from Newport with Cheese and Joe and a boy called Russell whom I've never seen before. Joe's been drinking, a bottle and half of wine according to reliable sources. He has been making us all laugh by telling us his babysitting stories. Apparently he found a stash of inappropriate magazines under the bed of a woman in the next road. I asked what he was doing looking under her bed and he said he always looks under people's beds. I'll tell you one thing. He's not babysitting for us.

I am going to go to bed myself now. Mummy is sitting in the kitchen with Cheese, telling her stories about you.

I love you so much. Sleep well, my angel.

Daddy

My darling,

Yet another Sunday and tomorrow another birthday.
Auntie Trish, Mel Bowe and Jill Wiggett all rang to ask
Mummy what she would like to do. She doesn't want to
do anything or see anybody. I have bought her a small
present which I think you would approve of: an antique
locket on a silver chain. It is quite big and later I am
going to find a picture of you to put inside it.

Last night we went to see John Keeling, and Jill and
Alan Wiggett came with us. We had intended only to stay
for an hour but we ended up leaving after midnight. John
had bought a whole range of Tesco Value snacks, which
were, for the most part, inedible but he had also stocked
up on wine and beer so we forgave him and pretended
that the sausage rolls were delicious. John's house is bright
and cosy and he had custody of both his daughters for the
weekend, which provided Horsey with some distraction.
Robbie had declined his invitation and chose to spend the
evening in Newport with Cheese. The conversation was
lively and for a while we laughed and lived in the
moment.

At around 9.00 p.m., two of John's neighbours turned
up, really nice people with whom we all felt comfortable

very quickly. The man, it transpired, was the son of a vicar which prompted Mummy to ask him whether he believed in God or in an afterlife. Neither the man nor his wife knew of our situation and we hardly rushed to say, 'Oh, by the way . . .' when they walked through the door. The man said that he didn't believe in God or an afterlife. 'When we die, we die,' he said. 'We get one chance so we had better make the most of it.' Mummy had had quite a lot to drink by this stage and I saw her chin fall and her hair drop, like a theatrical curtain, across her face. She had been holding court, her fragile good humour held in place by the warmth and friendship of the people around her. Whenever she sits down, one of her legs works like a trip hammer as if she is trying to win a sewing-machine race, but the more upset and desperate she becomes, the faster she taps her foot. We changed the subject and started talking about John's dodgy guitar playing but I could see that Mummy had lost her delicate grip on the evening and soon she made her excuses and disappeared to the loo. I knew she wouldn't come back so I went after her and found her crying on the stairs. 'Do you think he's right?' she said. 'Do you think there's nothing?' She could barely get the words out. 'He's a vicar's son. He must know.' I found myself crying too, not just for you but for Mummy and for myself. Sometimes I look at Mummy and it is as if she is fading away. In the depths of her misery, her beautiful face literally falls apart but her eyes are the worst. There is no light, no defiance. 'Do you believe?' she said. 'Do you believe in Charlie?'

And I do believe in you, darling. Every morning when I wake up, I say 'Good morning' to you. I go to the bathroom to wash and brush my teeth, and I look into your bedroom and again I say hello. I talk to you as I walk down the stairs and as I pour myself a bowl of cereal. I sit at the kitchen table and I kiss your picture. When I drive Robbie and Horsey to school, I talk about you. If there is a beautiful sky, I say Charlie would have loved that sky. If a herd of deer come to watch us on the top road to Newport, I say that you brought the deer just for us. I talk about you to Uncle Davy and to Oma and to Auntie Trish and I talk about you to everybody who knew you. I didn't use to do this. Up until about a week ago I couldn't do it. But the more I talk about you, the more I talk to you, the more real you seem to become. I went shopping today and I talked to you as I walked around the supermarket. I asked you which vegetables I should buy and, when I went through the frozen section, I let you decide. As a result I bought southern fried chicken wings and Ben and Jerry's ice cream, not to mention fresh cream scones and your favourite Caesar salad. I even bought Robbie some hot barbecued spare ribs. Instead of looking back, I'm trying to look forward and I'm taking you with me. So I told Mummy that I do believe in you because I do. I know that your spirit is watching me as I type. I don't know where you are and I don't necessarily believe in God but I believe in you and I believe in the spirits of all the lost children.

I miss your physical presence, your laughter, your beauty, your outrageous sense of humour, your courage, your stubbornness, the feel of your hand in mine, the smell of your breath in the morning. I miss your tears. You are my Charlie and I have three wonderful children and I will see you again.

Hello, my poppet,

I just stopped before. I didn't know what else to write. For a while I thought that I might have finished and that maybe I could carry on just by talking to you but yesterday, Mummy's birthday, was a nightmare and I felt all my brave words dissolve in a rain of tears. So many people came to see us or came to see Mummy anyway. Mel C and Harry Chapman arrived in the afternoon bearing flowers and chocolates. I cooked Harry a southern fried chicken wing and beans because he likes a meal and Mel C was bursting with energy and stories. In no time Paul and Mel Bowe and Beck turned up with wine and more flowers and then came Yvonne McPartland, and Jill Wiggett with Tom. In between, the phone didn't stop ringing. Auntie Jill called, and Toby and Patrick, and Cousin Kate and Roger.

Throughout it all Mummy drank more and more wine and I went out to buy an Indian takeaway for all the children, using one of the few credit cards I have left that haven't reached their limit. As the wine took hold, so Mummy's mood changed and soon we were left just with Jill and Tom. Horsey and Robbie stayed in the living room watching television. We had been swapping trivial stories about fat women and Alan's strange obsession with cleanliness, particularly his need to put everything he sees into black bin liners.

And then Mummy couldn't take it any more. I had been sitting on the kitchen floor with my back against the boiler, drinking tea and smoking, not really joining in much. 'My first birthday without Charlie,' I heard Mummy say. 'She loved my birthday. She would have cooked for me and made a special card and spent most of last week looking for just the right necklace and she would have insisted on opening all my presents because, to Charlie, all presents were her presents.' And Mummy was right because that is exactly what you would have done and you would have been holding court and laughing louder than anyone else and probably sitting in the middle of the table or on top of me on the floor, anywhere that afforded you maximum comfort whilst causing the maximum discomfort to others.

'I have to drink,' Mummy said. 'I have to drink or I can't sleep.' On Sunday night Mummy was awake again until 5 a.m., playing endless games of solitaire on the computer. And then she said something that she hasn't said before, not to me anyway. She said that she stays awake hoping that you will come to her and she knows that if it was possible for you to find a way, then you would come and that, because you haven't come, it means that there is nothing and there is no hope.

Roger, Uncle Davy, John Doe, all the people we know who have lost a child, they all tell us that they see signs. They talk about the white feather, rattling pipes, lights that

mysteriously turn themselves on and off, cars with bizarre
number plates, rainbows, animals: you name it, anything
can be a sign. We saw the most beautiful double rainbow
over the house only a few days ago. Adele saw the
rainbow just as her sister had suggested that your favourite
flower was the iris because Iris was the goddess of
rainbows. A few weeks ago the music box in the study
started playing on its own while I was at the computer.
I've never heard it make a sound before. I think it used to
belong to your great-grandmother and it has spent most of
its life at the bottom of a box in the garage. Sometime last
week I was awoken in the night by an enormous crash,
which seemed to have come from your room. I got up to
investigate and found nothing which was weird because it
sounded as if somebody had dropped an anvil through the
roof.

All these things could be signs but I have to believe in
them. Knowing you, I think that when you give us a sign
there won't be any room for doubt. You'll rearrange the
stars to spell out your name. And I do believe in you but
I know that it's up to me to make a leap of faith and if I
wait for proof, then I'll be waiting for the rest of my life.
This is what I tell Mummy and I tell her that we have to
believe in you because we can't take the chance. If you
are with us or watching over us, how will you be able to
bear it if we don't believe in you?

It's late on Tuesday evening. We returned about an hour
ago from taking Horsey to his final audition for Whizz

Kids. Whatever happens we are both so proud of him. You would have been with him. You should have been with him. While we were waiting for Horsey we went to Browns Restaurant for a drink. It is the most wonderful place, full of life, students and professors, passers-by and locals. Six girls sat at a table next to us. They were young, not as young as you, but no more than twenty. They had books with them and folders of typewritten sheets, and they were full of the promise of all that life has to offer. I used to dream that you would go to university in Cambridge, close enough to come home whenever you felt like it or for us to visit you or bring you food and supplies. In a few years it might have been you sitting together with your friends in Browns and maybe Mummy and I would still have looked young enough to sit near by and not embarrass you. All the shattered dreams. Life and death go on around us, unchecked.

Tomorrow the men from the Rail Accident Investigation Board are coming. I am dreading it. In the afternoon we were going to drive down to Devon to stay with Kate and Roger in their guest house which overlooks the sea. Insomuch as I look forward to anything, I was looking forward to it but Roger just rang to say that Uncle Ted has been taken ill and he may not survive the week. Both he and Kate are going to be at his bedside in Slough. I remember you sitting on Ted's lap when you were five and he told you stories about when he was a teacher and he would entertain his pupils by standing on his head in the classroom. I don't think there are any teachers like Ted any more.

I am tired now. My eyes are stinging. Mummy and Horsey are asleep in the sitting room and Robbie is upstairs in his room. I think he may be revising. Whatever he is doing, I am not going to disturb him. I am going to make myself a cup of tea and smoke a cigarette.

Bless you, my angel. Sleep well.

I love you.

Daddy

Hello, poppet,

It has been a long day. Spring appears to have scuttled back under a stone to make way for a last vicious blast of winter. Icy rain fell from a stormy sky punctured by rays of intermittent sun.

The men from the Rail Accident Investigation team came this morning. In my experience government officials all come from another planet where it is illegal not to eat pies whenever possible and be at least six feet two inches tall. Even drawing myself up to my full five feet eleven and half inches and puffing out my chest, I still felt like Gulliver in Brobdingnag. We crammed ourselves around the table in the kitchen, three men in dark suits and blue ties, all wearing serious yet understanding expressions. Peter, the policeman, was with them and he sat slightly to one side, his hands neatly folded in his lap. I am not sure whether he was there to protect them from me or me from them. One of the men introduced himself as the principal rail investigator and he went to some lengths to point out that he reported to the Minister for Transport and nobody else. He said that they had come in the main to listen to what I had to say but that they were not in a position to comment. I supposed that to mean that I could shout and scream at them and they wouldn't mind.

I didn't shout and scream but I told them what I think. I remembered everything. I told them that after nearly five months, the passenger gate remains open when a train is coming. That no ticket machine has been put on the northbound platform. That people still jump over the fence and run across the track to catch a train. I told them how appalled we are that we have heard nothing from Network Rail. In the end I suppose I found some comfort in the knowledge that the government have called for an independent inquiry and have not washed their hands of it and passed the buck to the rail operators. The RAIB, as they call themselves, cannot force changes on to the operators but they can make recommendations. If these recommendations are not acted upon, they can pass the case to Her Majesty's Rail Inspectorate which is like a court of appeal. This court can force change if it sees fit.

The large men in suits are definitely on our side even though they couldn't comment but nothing they or we do will bring you back. There are hundreds of crossings like the one at Elsenham in this country and they should all be made safe. The chief investigator said to me that all change comes about because of tragedy. In other words, because we have lost you, change will come about that will save lives but if you had lived the world might still be waiting for the death of another child before anything would be done. I think he thought that this might be comforting.

Why did it have to be you? Why does it ever have to

be anybody? It's about money. It always is. Why pay for something until you have to? If cars never crashed, they would be made of cardboard.

Because of the inquiry, your inquest might not be until the autumn at the earliest. Maybe as much as a year will pass before I have to sign the paper that makes what has happened to you official. A year before I can organise the stone for your grave.

Roger rang about an hour ago. Ted is a little better but he doesn't think it will be long before the inevitable happens. In two weeks' time it will be the first anniversary of Justin's death, Roger's son. Roger has quite a severe stammer but I don't really know him well enough to know whether he had a stammer before Justin died. Sometimes, for no obvious reason, I find that words get stuck in my mouth and I don't so much stammer as fail to speak altogether. Roger said that he and Kate have many good friends and they go out often, either to eat or just to the pub, and there are times when both he and Kate laugh and have a 'good' time but always, the next morning, he feels guilty and whether it is right to feel guilty or not, the guilt is inescapable. He said that he feels Justin is with him all the time and that his memories are becoming more vivid. My greatest fear now is that I will not be able to find you and that the rest of my life will pass without you in every sense of the word. Sometimes the harder I try to imagine you, the more elusive you become.

I talk to you more and more now. I walk around the house telling you how much I love you. I speak your name out loud where before I would whisper it. I realise that something is happening, that distance is altering my responses.

I love you darling. I will always love you. If you are watching me or you can somehow see inside my head, you know that I will always be with you and that love goes beyond the boundaries of the living.

Bless you, always.

Your Daddy

15 April 2006

Hello, poppet,

Two days have passed. I cannot remember what happened on Thursday. I think I did some work for David Rozalla, scanning and editing one of my father's books. Oh, I remember now. I was working on *The Montgomery Legend*, a book about Field Marshal Montgomery who commanded the British Forces in Africa in the Second World War, when Uncle Davy called and asked me to go to London to collect twenty tubs of mixed olives and some duck pâté. I took Horsey with me and he entertained me and distracted me by pretending to be sick and endlessly complaining about the traffic. We got home at around 7 p.m. and I just had time for a cup of tea before I had to go to Newport to pick up Robbie. Mummy was very low and we ended the evening in silence, drawn in by the whirlpool of loneliness that your absence creates.

Yesterday was Good Friday and we went to Sudbury to take part in the 'Do it for Dan' fun run. Uncle Davy and Auntie Trish told us that it would start at 10.30 a.m. and I was desperate to take part. Last year we ran together, you and I, even though neither of us had running shoes and, unlike all the other runners, I was wearing jeans and you were fully dressed and ran in your wellington boots. We came last but we still managed to run all the way and you kept me company although I am sure you could have finished in a much quicker time if you had wanted to. All the Wiggetts came too, giving up their holiday to raise money for the Hillside Special School and to honour your memory. Because Alan is organised and appreciates the importance of leaving time for things to go wrong, the Wiggetts arrived at 9.30, which was when the race actually started and, as a result, got to take part. We turned up at 10.30, just in time to greet the stragglers over the finishing line. It is typical of Uncle Davy not to know the start time of his own race. We went to Danny's Bar, which opened early and had turned itself into a coffee shop for the occasion. Auntie Trish was already there and Oma, and Chris and Lucy who seem to be omnipresent at all family get-togethers. Uncle Davy walked the course wearing a white chef's jacket, a panama hat and Cuban-heeled boots. Alan Wiggett commented that he thought Uncle Davy's fancy dress was really inventive, unaware that Uncle Davy dresses like that all the time.

Sometimes I can't cope with other people. I found that I couldn't sit in the bar and talk aimlessly about nothing. Mummy found herself wedged between Auntie Trish and Lucy but with the aid of tobacco and several strong cups of coffee, she endured while I quietly excused myself and walked around the town. I held your hand and talked to you and we sat together on a bench on the market hill and watched people coming and going. Presently Uncle Davy found us and we sat side by side in the watery spring sunshine. There wasn't anything to say. Uncle Davy misses Dan just as I miss you.

Later on we all went back to Southfork and the Wiggetts came too. We sat on the patio and Auntie Trish cooked huge plates of sausages and fried chicken along with bowls of salad and garlic bread. Uncle Davy, who is allergic to food that he hasn't cooked himself, rustled up a special pasta dish which he let me have some of, and we drank Somerfield's own best bitter and red wine. You would have loved it. We have hardly been to Southfork at all since Christmas. One of my great pleasures in going there was to bathe in the afterglow of your excitement, especially in the summer when the pool was open and you could run around the garden in your swimming costume, leaping in and out of the pool on a whim, splashing through Auntie Trish's beautiful kitchen which was something only you could get away with.

This is the first year when we haven't had an Easter egg hunt. Horsey didn't complain and Robbie has reached the stage where he regards Easter egg hunts with contempt. He believes that hunting for an Easter egg is a contradiction. He should be able to find them and eat them with the minimum of fuss. Last Easter seems like yesterday. It was raining, I remember, and I had to walk around the garden at Southfork with a carrier bag full of creme eggs, hiding them in every available flowerpot and crevice, under the eaves of the roof, in the handles of the wheelbarrow, in with the fish food by the pond, anywhere that would provide you with a challenge. I did try to get out of it, saying that Easter egg hunts didn't really work in the rain, but you were unimpressed and made your feelings known with a simple look. If you found all the eggs too quickly, you would always make me hide them again.

I sat at the table on the patio and watched you in my mind, looking in all the usual places, fighting with Horsey if you both happened upon a hiding place at the same time, running from the bottom of the garden to show me how many you had found. I cannot escape the feeling that life is no longer real.

I was listening to the radio the other day and I overheard an interview with a man called Norman Kember who was kidnapped and held for several months in Iraq. It must have been terrible for him, each day coming and going with the threat of a violent death ever present. He broke down in tears on a number of occasions but what really struck me was when he said that his life no longer seemed real. In our different ways, Mr Kember, Mummy, all of us, have suffered unspeakable trauma. Life can never be the same and it may never seem real again.

Tonight we are going to dinner with Paul and Mel. Paul has promised to cook their special vegetable lasagne. Mummy doesn't really want to go but I hope that once she is there, the warmth of the company and the change in surroundings will provide some solace.

Chelsea won again.

I love you darling.

Your Daddy

Sweetheart,

I meant to tell you that when the post came on
Saturday we received a letter from the chief executive of
Network Rail, a man called John Armitt. I sat by the
front door holding the thing in my hands for God
knows how long without opening it. I don't know what
I expected it to say but I am terrified by these cold
islands of reality. The men from the RAIB, the
occasional calls from the police liaison officer, official
letters. They all catapult me back to that day, the
memory of which becomes more unbearable and not less
so. Eventually I opened it, tearing it across the top, my
hands shaking. Inside there were two sheets of A4. Mr
Armitt offered us his condolences which was nice of
him. I don't suppose Network Rail or Mr Armitt would
have written had there not been pressure from the RAIB
and the lawyers. The letter says that we should meet
Network Rail to 'determine whether any changes can be
made to this crossing in the future'. What are they
waiting for? Do they want somebody else to die or
perhaps your life and Livvy's life weren't enough? The
fury I feel at what this man has to say leaves me
speechless. I will write back but not yet. I have learnt

enough to know that if my anger is uncontrolled we have less chance of achieving anything.

In the same post a letter came from the lawyers saying that Network Rail had at last responded to the letter of claim. They will make their case within three months. My hatred has hardened and it sits inside me like the stone of a rotten fruit.

Yesterday was Easter Sunday. All I really wanted to do was walk up to the church and light a candle for you and perhaps sit in one of the pews and find some peace. I stare at the stained-glass windows, at finely detailed pictures of friars and monks, painstakingly assembled in a myriad of colours. They all look so pious to me, their rich robes and sober faces, heads tilted towards the heavens. I find no comfort in them but the Reverend Titford is right about the church. There is a sense of protective timelessness.

I forgot to go shopping so we had very little food. I went to the Spar and bought chicken breasts in breadcrumbs and oven chips for Robbie and Horsey. I can't remember whether Mummy and I ate anything. I suppose we must have done but I can't remember what. Uncle Davy called in the evening, unable to escape from his own misery. I found myself trying to comfort him. Later I called Oma who asked whether we had been listening to the Pope. I never listen to the Pope but I let Oma down gently. I said that we had been to church, which seemed to satisfy her.

I don't know how I am feeling any more. I am lost but being lost has become almost normal. The physical pain has mostly disappeared. I don't feel sick very often and the knot in my stomach is noticeable now only when it is there and not when it is gone, as before.

I am, in a strange kind of way, quite busy. I have some sort of routine. When Robbie and Horsey are at school, I clean the house in the morning and wash up from the night before. I make myself toast and read the paper and I look forward to a cup of tea and a first cigarette. Later I write and in the afternoon I scan and edit your grandfather's books for David Rozalla's website. I have also started to prepare notes for the lectures that I have to give at Saffron Walden County High School. I had thought that Robbie and Horsey would be horribly embarrassed by the thought of my trying to become a teacher but they have taken it very well. Robbie thinks I will be fine and Horsey is sure that most of the students will be physically sick when they see me. The first lecture is still ten days away so I have not started to feel nervous yet. I know, at least, that you would be stricken by the idea. 'No, Daddy,' you would have said. 'Please don't do it. I know people at the County High. Clare McPartland goes there.' On the day of the lecture you would have prostrated yourself in front of the door to prevent me from leaving or wrapped yourself around one of my legs and forced me to drag you down the hall. It wouldn't have been beyond you to steal my car keys and throw them in the pond.

I miss you so much. I miss the noise and anarchy, the sudden, spontaneous laughter, the disconnected shriek that let us all know that Horsey had trodden on your toe or accidentally on purpose poked you in the eye with a pencil. Memories of you play like miniature movies in my head. I see you sitting on the arm of the settee, aimlessly swinging your leg. Eating with your fingers, but so delicately, like some ancient Roman goddess with your little finger raised.

I played catch with Horsey earlier, outside in the road just as we did last summer. You would come out and join us after five minutes or so and stand in front of the garage with your hands in your pockets. I would throw the ball to you and more often than not, it would hit you in the chest or bounce off your head as you made no attempt whatsoever to catch it. Then you would shake your head and stare at me as if I was an idiot. 'Why did you throw the ball to me?' you would say. 'I'm *obviously* not playing. Why do you think I've got my hands in my pockets?' Sometimes I used to get annoyed and you would flounce back into the house and ignore me when I came in. You could be so obtuse.

I remember telling you that losing you might in some way be similar to having a limb amputated in the sense that I simply can't believe that you are not here. I can't believe that you are not in the next room doing your homework. I can't believe that the next sound of a key turning in the lock won't be you.

I found some more pictures of you taken when we lived in Mill Road in Henham. You were three. I am looking at one of the pictures now with a sense of wonder. You are wearing grey pyjama bottoms with red squares on them and a red sweatshirt with the word TRADER printed in an arc across your chest. Your hair is down to your shoulders and curling under your cheeks which are two big, red spots, and I can see your dimples. You are looking down with your mouth drawn up in a faint smile and your eyes are closed. I would scoop you up in my arms and you would cling to me and when you felt safe, you would lean back and survey all that you owned.

I realise that throughout your life I always expected you to be there but you were a gift that I should have savoured for every moment. Perhaps I am lucky to be your father, to have been blessed for thirteen, short years. But my heart is broken for you. For all the things that you will never do. For all the things that you will never see. These are the thoughts that I cannot bear.

Hello, sweetheart,

The longest time has passed since I last wrote to you.
Ten days. I was beginning to think that I might not write
again. It will be Saturday tomorrow. Five months, 150
days since I last held you in my arms. I think of you all
the time and even when I am consciously doing
something else, I am aware of you. I know it is the same
for Mummy.

She has started again at the school whereas only a month
ago she said that she thought she would never be able to go
back. Her friend Karen, whom you knew, has never given
up on her, coaxing her and refusing to take no for an
answer. On her first day back, Mummy came home with at
least six boxes of chocolates and two bunches of flowers.
She talked about the children for nearly an hour, about how
so many of them had hugged her and about a little boy who
is partially autistic who came up to her and said: 'Was it
your daughter who was killed by the train?' I shuddered
when she repeated the words and looked away. I find that I
can barely write the words and I know that I will never be
able to say them. I wondered how Mummy had been able
to bear it but she said that she had been fine, it was as if the
boy had been talking about someone else. Then the same

little boy went up to Philippa, one of the other teachers and said: 'Mrs Thompson is very strong.' Mummy said that Philippa was surprised but before she had time to answer, the boy continued. 'Yes,' he said, 'she can lift a whole stack of chairs.'

People keep telling Mummy how proud they are of her, how courageous she is to go back to work, but Mummy is baffled. She says that she doesn't feel brave at all, that she had no choice because to have stayed at home would have driven her mad. Here she is trapped by her guilt and her memories. I try to talk to her, to tell her that she has nothing to feel guilty about, but nothing I can say will make any difference. She would go back in time and undo all the times when either of us might have turned you away or stopped you from doing what you wanted. She doesn't understand why sometimes she minded you wearing her clothes or her frustration at your decisions to wear five different outfits in one day, creating huge piles of washing and the prospect of long evenings shackled to the ironing board. I am not sure if it is the same for Mummy as it is for me, but I cannot choose my memories. They come tumbling, unbidden, out of nowhere. I still feel the guilt of two Christmases ago when, driven to the brink of reason, I smacked you in the same way that you sometimes see in films, when one character slaps another around the face to bring them to their senses. You never forgave me for it and I never forgave myself. You teased me, threatening to report me to the Social Services, and I often worried that, in some mad, hormonal moment, you might actually do it.

Changes keep coming. I know that our life was not perfect. I know that we rowed and there were times when you went to your room in tears and both of us, imprisoned by our stubbornness, found it impossible to apologise. Evenings ruined by your natural childishness and my inability to grow up. I know that I adore you and that I will always adore you. You were like the sun. You dazzled everyone you met. I spent thirteen years captivated by your brilliance and your image has been burnt, forever, into my brain.

Mummy is right. Our lives ended when you died. We have started again and our new life is beginning to take hold. Horsey has joined the local cricket club and we have been to nets four times in the last week. Robbie, still tortured and occasionally inconsolable, has imperceptibly realised that he needs to do at least some work to secure his place in the sixth form and Cheese helps him, leading by example. You are always with us, your absence a tangible thing. I talk to you all the time now. I no longer feel self-conscious because I think that was part of my problem. Mummy says that you have been frozen in time, captured for ever at the crossroads of innocence and experience. You will never grow old.

It has been the most beautiful day. I drove to Sudbury this morning to see Oma and Uncle Davy. Oma has rewritten the foreword for your grandfather's website and I promised to call in to see Uncle Davy to share a cup of tea and a cigarette and talk briefly about Charlie's Larder. I drove with the window down and my sleeves rolled up, feeling the almost warm breeze in my face. The hedgerows are full of hawthorn. Thomas Hardy described hawthorn as 'bosky' and I cannot think of a better word. Cowslips line the verges, their trumpet flowers heralding the onset of summer. It has been the sort of day when I used to think it would be impossible to feel sad. You would have been sitting next to me, holding my hand while leaning out of the window, letting the wind blow back your hair. I wonder now whether I will ever feel happy again or whether the memory of once being happy will be enough.

I know now that I may not write again for a while. You have heard enough of our misery. Sometimes I am sure that you are there, watching over us. Uncle Davy has what he calls his 'Dan time' when he needs to be alone, to think of Dan, to try to make sense of what has happened. For me and for Mummy, I think, all our time is for you. I have dreams still. I want to travel, to go to places where I can perhaps more easily believe that there is something else. I want Horsey and Robbie to find the right path to a fulfilling life and I want to be there for them, to help them when they need me. I find any kind of long-term future harder to imagine. I may die tomorrow but I might also live for another thirty or even forty years. What kind of an old man am I going to be, deprived of my daughter for such a terrible length of time? When Robbie and Horsey have finally left home, what are Mummy and I going to do in the long evenings? Mummy says that she believes that you will be waiting for us. I want to believe that too.

I long for you, my darling. When I am ready I will write again.

Night-night, sleep well. We will come up and see you.

Your Daddy

My darling,

Nearly a month has passed since my last letter. So much has happened. I have been writing to you in my head every day, making sure not to miss anything out. It is Sunday morning. Mummy is in the kitchen reading the paper. I can hear the rustle as she turns the page. Horsey is still asleep in the living room and Robbie stayed in Newport with Cheese last night. For once the sun is shining but it has rained almost continuously for the last two weeks. All around us the full force of summer has taken hold. The chestnut trees seem to sag under the burden of their leaves and cow parsley overflows the hedge rows. I am astounded by nature's perfection. The flawless yellow of countless fields of rape seed, the perfect variations of green, making each tree an individual.

Yesterday I drove back from Newport after dropping Robbie off outside the Londis. I was trying to understand why I never feel quite prepared for the abundance of summer. Does nature mourn the death of last year's flowers?

It was six months yesterday. Six months since I last saw you. Mummy dreamt about you last night. She said that she could feel your skin, touch your hair, that you were real even though, in her dream, you were wearing an orange tracksuit. She was standing with her back to me, leaning forwards, using both her hands to balance herself against the rim of the cooker. I knew that she was crying even though there was no sound and no sign of any convulsion, no sudden, deeper intake of breath. The tears run silently for both of us. I hugged Mummy. She lets me hug her now but there are still no words I can think of to comfort her.

I remember when I rang the woman from Compassionate Friends sometime back in January and she said to me that she was surprised that I should call so soon after the accident. Most people don't call for at least six months, she said. I didn't understand then. I rang because I didn't know what to do. I wanted to find somebody who would tell me that you were fine, that you are in heaven, that your spirit exists and that this life is just a stage, one step in an endless series of evolutionary leaps. Of course the woman to whom I spoke could tell me nothing of what I wanted to hear. Now I understand better why people don't ring until about now.

Life on the surface has resumed a kind of routine normality. Mummy has been back at work for two months. I have completed my five lectures at the County High. Robbie has started his GCSEs. Horsey has already played three times for the Thaxted under-fifteens cricket team. Paul and Mel visit once a week or so and the Wiggetts come often although with a greater randomness. Mummy speaks daily on the phone to Jill and Mel B and Yvonne, Charlie McP's mother, who has become a good friend and a tireless supporter in the fight against Network Rail. Adele still comes on most Fridays, always with home-made soup and a handful of freshly laid eggs, and Robbie's band practice is a staple of Saturday afternoons. Murray and John Keeling and David Rozalla stay in touch. John worries about my appearance and my inability to arrive anywhere on time. With everything that has happened, he fears that my lack of professionalism will count against me.

I laugh, I tell jokes and my mask, for the most part, stays firmly in place but the skin, the eyes, the nose that everybody else sees is not my face. I feel that I am about to cry at any moment and sometimes, when I am alone, I take the mask off and the tears come and my real face twists in agony.

Hello, poppet,

I meant to come back to the computer yesterday but we went to Cambridge to see *X-Men 3* and to buy Robbie and Horsey some clothes. Robbie has been reduced to wearing a pair of jeans at mid-thigh level to ensure that the legs are long enough to cover the tops of his trainers. The trainers themselves, bought at huge expense about three months ago on the internet and designed, according to Robbie, by the lead guitarist of Blink 182, had started to come apart at the seams, the soles peeling away from the rest of the shoes with a suspicious symmetry. Horsey is growing faster than a giant redwood, which is the fastest-growing tree but has the smallest seed, roughly one billionth the size of the fully grown parent. I learn these amazing facts from watching late-night television.

The film was terrible. The entire cast looked as if they had been kidnapped by a mutant hairdresser. We got back quite late and Mummy beat me to the computer. She has become obsessed by e-mails and sits, gazing blankly at the screen, waiting for them to arrive. She prefers a message from a friend but any old spam will do.

There are so many things I need to tell you but I don't

quite know where to start. Robbie sat his first GCSE last Tuesday. It was ICT. I have never been entirely sure what ICT stands for and the fact that Robbie is not sure either doesn't fill me with confidence. I persuaded him to do some revision the day before and he went on to a website called Bitesize and learnt all sorts of obscure facts that sounded really impressive. Afterwards Robbie told me that not a single thing he revised came up in the exam but nonetheless he had managed to answer all the questions without understanding any of them. On the following day he took his French oral. I am pretty sure he actually went to the exam and these days you get half the marks for just turning up. He has nothing else now until next Monday and he has promised to 'cram as he has never crammed before'. I pointed out to him that he has never crammed before and he fixed me with the one-eyed stare that he reserves for moments of extreme inscrutability and said, 'Exactly.'

It's just after 5 p.m. on Monday afternoon. It's raining as usual. We get interludes of sun for fifteen minutes or so at two-hour intervals while sinister purple and black clouds gather themselves over the church spire. Mummy is asleep on the settee in the living room and Horsey has been reading a game-roleplaying book given to him by an old friend of ours who came to visit on Friday night.

I took Robbie to Newport but only after we had another row. He hates me going into his room but he never cleans it and no matter how many times Mummy and I ask, he never brings us his dirty clothes. I went in this morning to clear out the debris from the night before:

half-drunk glasses of Coke, bits of old biscuit, a white
cereal bowl full of congealed custard. I found a small pile
of tobacco on his desk all mixed up with cannabis leaves.
I know he smokes dope sometimes. I wish he didn't but
it's like a plague. At least he doesn't drink and he seems to
be smoking less but I am terrified where drugs might lead.
I told him I wouldn't have it in the house and that I had
asked him not to do it at all. He said that everybody in
his year smokes dope and he smokes much less than most.
I told him I didn't care about the others. What they do is
their business. We ended up screaming at each other,
slamming doors so hard that the screws holding the
handles on flew out on to the floor.

I hate shouting. I hate losing control. I remember when
I would get so angry with you, for some reason most
often when we were in the car together, and the shame
that I felt when the anger passed. I remember you sitting
next to me in the passenger seat and calling me a bastard
with a look of utter hate in your eyes. I would leave you
in the car, going into the house on the verge of tears. For
me the anger would dissolve in minutes. Then I would go
back out to find you and I would try to take you in my
arms and cuddle you and tell you I was sorry even though
the row had probably been your fault. It's the same with
Robbie. I get too angry so that I feel guilty and end up
saying sorry to him.

Mummy can't bear it. Each day is hard enough as it
is. Horsey sits cross-legged on the living room floor,
reading his book, hearing everything. After the row with
Robbie, he came up to me and cuddled me, wrapping

his arms around my waist and burying his head in my stomach.

We've run out of pills again. I am definitely less able to cope without them. They don't make me happier or even dull the pain, they simply act as a kind of brake.

Mrs Wiggett just rang. She and Alan are coming round in an hour. I didn't put them off because they will distract Mummy and Mrs Wiggett is a bottomless well of gossip and funny stories. She bought a leopardskin dress last week, which she blamed on you. She said that she had gone shopping in Cambridge with the intent to buy some demure get-up for work and that you had suddenly popped up beside her and forced her to buy a ridiculous dress. She said that it was entirely your fault and that she had never bought anything else remotely like it in her life. She brought it round in a carrier bag and tried to palm it off on Mummy. I think it's got something to do with her new job, working in the 'Big and Fat' department at Pearsons in Bishop's Stortford. She has taken to walking round the market place on Saturdays offering potential customers free cream buns.

It's 4.30 p.m. on Tuesday. A day and half has passed. The Wiggetts came and went, briefly lighting up the day. I have never told you this before but Alan and Tom are mad keen fishermen, or anglers, as they prefer to be called. Tom nearly won a regional angling contest and Alan caught a twenty-six-pound carp in Henham Lake. Sometimes Alan will take Tom and they will fish through the night. I had this image of them, sitting silently on the river bank, silhouetted by the light of the moon, utterly

still and ghostly, their bodies half hidden by torn remnants
of mist, but apparently the truth is very different. They
have a top of-the-range tent with space-age sleeping bags,
the sort that mountaineers use halfway up Everest, and
they take a picnic hamper and flasks of tea. They turn in
at around 10 p.m., probably with a good book, and
meanwhile their rods are linked to alarms in the tent
which go off when they get a bite. I was a bit
disappointed. It seemed to take the romance out of it.
Alan had a ridiculous picture of himself holding his record
catch. It was the fattest fish I had ever seen. It looked as if
it had been force-fed pies since birth.

After the Wiggetts left, the silence, which had been
pushed temporarily to the corners of the room, crept back
and devoured us.

Yesterday I spent the morning paying bills and then
Mummy and I went to look at a house in Newport. We
have sold this house at last and suddenly we have only a
month to find somewhere else. I haven't really been
paying attention and I have felt no need for urgency.
Much as we can't stay here, neither Mummy nor I have
any enthusiasm for another home. We are going to try to
find a place in Newport because it will be near to the
school and near to Robbie and Horsey's friends. The
house we went to see was small but clean with three
bedrooms, which is all we need now. When the estate
agent asks how many bedrooms we are looking for, I
struggle to say three. It is as if by doing so I am denying
your existence. It is like telling people who might need to
know that we have only two children but if I say that we

have three, then I have to say what happened and I don't
feel comfortable burdening strangers with our grief.
Anyway the house was no good. The main train line to
Cambridge ran through the back of the garden. Once it
wouldn't have bothered me. It is amazing what good
double glazing can do but now I cannot look at a train
and the idea of living with them is beyond horror.

Later on I played catch with Horsey in the garden.
You'll be really annoyed to hear how good he is. I think
he may be the only Thompson with any kind of aptitude
for sport. I will never forget going with Mummy to watch
you play rugby when you were in your last year at
Henham. I found the whole idea of girls being forced to
play rugby a little bit odd but that's probably something to
do with my age and some outmoded idea that rugby is
quite violent, dirty and smelly, and played by people for
whom the word baggy has no meaning. I remember
watching you in awe as the game went on around you
and you stood in the centre circle, talking to Leanna. You
looked fantastic in your brand-new blue and white
chequered rugby shirt with your hair in a ponytail.
Occasionally the ball would come towards you and you
showed tremendous agility, leaping out of the way at the
last moment before resuming your conversation. They
never asked you to play again. At least Mummy didn't
have to wash your kit.

I took Robbie and Cheese into Newport about two
hours ago. They had been revising all afternoon.
Notwithstanding the rows or the dope, I am so proud of
Robbie. He has found the strength from somewhere to

carry on at school, even to apply himself to his work, albeit in a haphazard kind of way. Most of his friends drink and smoke, and Robbie is by far from being the worst offender. He plays the guitar beautifully, his fingers moving effortlessly over the frets. At the last band practice I stood outside the door listening. They sound like a proper band and virtually all of their songs are original. Even Charlie McP's singing is improving. Well, he still can't sing but he talks loudly in all the right places.

Earlier on in the afternoon we went to see another house, this time to rent and not buy. It's at the top of School Lane, so close to the school that it could be linked by an adjoining door. Robbie didn't come with us and neither did Horsey who's been at Billy's all day, but it's within staggering distance of virtually all of Robbie's friends and Billy too, who still hasn't reached staggering age. The house has three bedrooms and an attic room and the most fantastic kitchen I have ever seen, big enough to play cricket in but still cosy. While the woman was showing us round I found myself unable to bear it. You would love this house so much. One of the bedrooms is painted totally pink, the walls, the ceiling, the light fittings, everything. It is your room. It has a window looking out over the garden and beneath the window there is a sloping, tiled roof, part of the kitchen extension, meaning that you could have climbed out of the window and dropped down on to the grass without anybody knowing. I stood halfway up the stairs, tears running down my face, knowing that this is the house that you would have loved more than any other. How can we live in it without you? We told the woman we wanted the house and we may hear tomorrow, then we walked back to the car. We didn't say a word. On the drive back home Mummy leant against the door with her hand covering her face.

I told Robbie about the house, about the room for you because he will want the attic room. He stood in the doorway between the kitchen and the hall, pressing himself against the frame of the door so that I could see only half his face. His face was so white and the one eye that I could see had a desperate sadness. I asked him whether he was OK and he said that he was and then he asked whether I could take him to Newport. Cheese was upstairs and Mummy was on the computer so we were alone. I tried to hug him which is like trying to hug a plank, but suddenly he relaxed and pushed his face into my neck. He didn't cry and then he said to me that he hadn't wanted to move into a house without a room for you but he hadn't known how to tell us because he knew we couldn't afford a house with four bedrooms. I told him that we would take everything of yours and put your posters up and fill the cupboards with your clothes and leave your shoes in random places all over the house. We will take you with us wherever we go. You are part of this family. You will always be part of this family.

Horsey just came home. I let him in and he accidentally headbutted me on the bridge of the nose. I am going to watch *Celebrity X Factor* with Mummy now.

I love you so much.

Bless you my darling.

Daddy

Hello, my sweetheart,

Late again. Robbie went to London today, shopping with Cheese. Mummy gave her £50 towards a prom dress because her mother, Catherine, has no money and works all hours just to survive. In the day she fills in as an auxiliary nurse at the local hospital and in the evening she drives a taxi. We have no money either but with the sale of the house we will be able to pay off our debts and have a little over to start again.

I went to see Oma today. She took me to lunch at the Fox in Bulmer which you and I delivered to together in Uncle Davy's van. We both had huge rump steak burgers with a side order of asparagus. Oma took nearly two hours to eat a quarter of her burger and then pronounced it cold and sent it back. I didn't say anything. Neither of us can cope with any more rows.

We talked about Davy and Trish and the fact that they seem to be unable to comfort each other. They both grieve in such different ways. Trish buries her emotions below the surface and, to the outside world, appears to carry on as if nothing had ever happened. I know how much she hurts and sometimes, when we talk, she peels back the bandage and I can see that the wound is still raw.

Even though it is now eighteen months since Dan died, Uncle Davy sinks lower into a desolation of regret and misery. When I see him, he says immediately that he knows it must be worse for me but I have Mummy and Robbie and Horsey, and we share our grief, clinging to each other when we most need to. Davy seems to find no comfort in his children and maybe none in Trish but she in turn finds no comfort in him. My heart is broken for them too.

I was loading the dishwasher earlier and found myself methodically turning all the knives so that the sharp ends were pointing downwards. I remember reading a long time ago a tragic story about a little boy who was killed when he tripped and fell into an open dishwasher. So random, so utterly pointless. For years I have carefully put the covers back on to my used razors after Horsey cut himself sticking his hand into the toothbrush jar in the bathroom. Obviously I used to discard my old razors anywhere in those days. Everything I did, everything I still do, is to protect you all. It's an obsession. We've always been so terrified that anything would happen to any of you.

The summer before last, I used to take you into Bishop's Stortford to be with your friends on a Saturday morning and I would drop you outside that hideous cinema complex with the bowling alley and the McDonald's, and Mummy used to panic because there are always fights there, although mostly after dark, and I used to force you to sit in the car while I delivered my safety lecture. Don't talk to strangers. Don't wave your money about in public. Don't cross the road without looking. And once or twice I actually said to you that if anything happened to you, our lives would be over. Then you would get out of the car and give me your most withering look as if I was some kind of deranged halfwit, but I would still sit and watch you for a couple of minutes, chatting with your friends, oblivious to me and everything else around you. I never felt truly happy unless you were at home where I could see you.

It's 10.20 p.m. Soon I will have to go and get Robbie. He rang when he got back to Newport. I asked him about his day in London and whether Cheese had bought a dress.

Cheese bought the dress and Robbie had a rotten time. It rained and he spent three hours in Topshop.

I love you, darling. I can't not think about you. Not talk to you. Not write to you. I can't let this new life become normal.

Bless you. Sleep well.

Daddy

Poppet,

It's past midnight. Mummy is in the living room watching *Dalziel and Pascoe.* Horsey is asleep and Robbie is in his room. He has been revising for most of the day and Cheese says that he is better at maths than she is, which is saying something, given that she's brilliant at everything.

Mel Bowe rang earlier, inviting us to join them at the Rhodes Hall in Bishop's Stortford to enjoy an evening of African tribal chanting. I heard Mummy on the phone. Quick as a flash she said that I was ill and incapable of leaving the house but otherwise we would have loved to have gone. I don't think Mel fell for it. She and Paul were only going because the event was organised by the organisation for which she works. We haven't seen them for nearly two weeks and I miss them. I miss Paul's remarkable good nature and gentleness and his ability to find humour in almost anything. And sometimes it is relaxing just to listen to Mel talk. An evening with Mel requires almost no effort. You need merely to sit, listen, drink and occasionally nod.

Mrs Wiggett has invited us to watch England play football tomorrow afternoon. She has promised to burn some pizzas for us at half-time.

It is very quiet now. I am staring at the picture of you that is stuck to the wall above my desk with some Blu-tack. I've got two pictures of you actually. One is stuck above the other. The top one is like a cameo. You are wearing Mummy's dark glasses and you look as if you should be drinking champagne on the deck of a yacht in the South of France while a man in a dark suit and a peaked cap unloads your luggage from the boot of a Rolls-Royce. Mummy has found some more pictures of you and lined them up on the mantelpiece. Sometimes I will just sit and stare at them, trying to remember the exact moment, trying to bring it to life in my head. There is one when you were about two and I think it was taken in Winch and Blatch, which is a department store in Sudbury. I can see the room in which the picture was taken. I can even see the photographer's face but I can't feel anything. I can't feel your hand in mine. I can't hear your voice. The memory itself is two-dimensional. Flat. A picture in a picture. I don't even know whether I was happy or sad, irritable or relaxed.

When I think of the last times we had together, you are alive. I can hear your voice. Feel your skin. Smell your breath as you sleep.

So much has happened. The first report into your accident has been published. It has been compiled by the RSSB (The Rail Safety and Standards Board). Nobody bothered to send us a copy but Paul rang and directed me to the relevant site on the internet. The full report is fifty-six pages long. I read all of it, every clause, even the small print. It was like having an out-of-body experience. I found that a part of me was looking down on myself, sitting in front of the computer screen, reading this cold, analytical, emotionless document written and researched to inform strangers of the circumstances of your accident and the reasons for it. In the end it concludes that there are nine recommendations for improvements that could be made at Elsenham station to improve the overall level of safety. It also concludes that the accident was essentially your own fault. You didn't understand the sequence of the miniature red warning lights. The report calls them MWLs. I was on page thirty-eight before I worked out what MWLs stood for. There is no glossary at the back to explain terms. The report expects its readers to understand. You died because you didn't know that if the lights continue to flash after a train has arrived at the station, it means another train is coming. I didn't know that either. If I had been with you, I would be dead too.

The safety improvements outlined by the report are only recommendations. Network Rail doesn't have to act if it doesn't want to. The company may believe that its money is better spent giving bonuses to its executive staff. Somewhere in the report there is what is called 'a table of fatalities'. It lists in numerical terms the numbers of people killed and injured on the railways and in what circumstances. For example: people killed on unmanned level crossings since 1998. People killed and injured crossing the tracks where they may be designated as a public footpath. People killed and injured in collisions. On it goes. You died at a manned level crossing, which is very rare. Too rare for the statistics to alarm the planners.

It doesn't say how many children have to die before there is a need to take action. Ten? Twenty?

We live in a country where playing conkers has been banned in school playgrounds because of potentially fatal bruised knuckles. Kites have been banned from beaches because a woman got her legs tangled up in a guide rope and nearly fell over. Nobody's allowed to smoke any more because non-smokers may contract a fatal disease, but children are allowed to run across busy railway tracks because bridges cost money.

I'm sorry, darling. I'm so terribly sorry.

I can't sleep. I don't want to sleep. I don't want to lie in the dark with my eyes open watching you walk out on to that track. I am going to make myself another cup of tea and smoke a roll-up. I've had enough now. I want you to come home.

Darling one,

I didn't write yesterday. We went to the Wiggetts' to watch the football as promised. Mrs Wiggett let us down when it came to the pizzas. There were no pizzas to be seen, burnt or otherwise. Instead, carefully laid out on the table and covered with individual segments of kitchen towel, was a collection of wooden bowls, each containing a different delicacy. Cheese slices. Tesco Value ham (thinly sliced). Skips (prawn cocktail flavour) and some junior Melton Mowbray pork pies. I could see who had done the shopping. If Alan had been to the supermarket, we would have been tucking into a selection of Tesco's Finest, everything from onion bhajis to crab sticks with a few olives thrown in for good measure.

England won the match 6–0, which was significantly more boring than it sounds. For every goal we scored, the opposition kicked the ball into its own net to even things up.

Mummy sat outside with Mrs Wiggett and Horsey played a game on Harry Wiggett's computer. We didn't stay very late. Once all the cheese slices had gone, it was time to go. I was expecting to pick Robbie up sometime later but in the end he stayed at Cheese's house and only returned this afternoon.

When we got home Horsey and I watched *Daredevil* on television and Mummy played cards. We still sleep in the living room. I think Mummy would sleep upstairs but I can't. I haven't been into your room for two months. I find it hard even to look through the door. Your school shoes still sit neatly side by side at the foot of the wardrobe. There are two pink storage boxes in the middle of the floor, which I think Mummy pulled out from under your bed. I don't know what's in them. There's a DVD on the top of your chest of drawers which I should have taken back to Blockbuster. It was the last film you watched, *The Princess Diaries 2*. I don't know why I can't go into your room. I have to steel myself just walking towards your door when I go to see Robbie. There's another pair of your shoes in the downstairs loo. Sometimes I stare at them. I have never thought of shoes as being empty before. Your shoes are empty. Your clothes are empty.

I'm just sitting here now, looking at the screen. Nothing is in my head. I can hear Mummy on the telephone, the end of each word a whispered hiss, which somehow carries through the wall. Robbie emerged from his room and noisily ate a packet of crisps while standing in the doorway. Horsey is watching *South Park* again although he rushed out to tell me it was a 'nice' episode.

A boy died today, killed on his motorbike on the road from Thaxted to Dunmow. He was a friend of the curly-haired boy who works behind the bar in the Swan. Mummy told me after supper. We were standing in the kitchen, staring out into the garden, each smoking a cigarette. Mummy started crying. Another family shattered. Another pointless death. Last week more than 5,000 people died in an earthquake in Java. I don't know at what time of day it happened. Maybe they were all having their breakfast when the ground opened up and swallowed them. I haven't watched the news for several days. Many more will have died. Soldiers in Iraq, children in Africa. Death is everywhere. I read in a book today that in the last ten years, an estimated 3 million cricket balls have been lost in hedges and ditches surrounding rural English cricket pitches. According to the author this equates to somewhere in the region of 3,000 tons of balls lying unnoticed right in front of our very eyes.

We only notice death when it slaps us in the face but it is all around us, under our feet, in the next house, waiting at the bus stop. It sits at the bar while we talk and make our plans for tomorrow. Why did Death sit down next to you?

I'm going to see Doctor Tayler in the morning. It must be six weeks since I've seen him. I'm going to ask him to do some tests. Blood, blood pressure, that kind of thing. Part of me thinks 'what does it matter if I am ill,' but the rational, sensible part of my brain, if such a thing exists, knows that I still have a family to care for, a responsibility too great to abandon. Mummy wants me to ask him whether he thinks it is too late for us to have another baby. We haven't really talked very much about such a possibility. Mummy just wants to know, that's all.

I love you darling. I have to keep saying it. I say, 'I love you,' when I get up in the morning. I say I love you when I am sitting at the kitchen table with your pictures. I have found a third to go with the one taken in Brighton last summer and the one of you and Beck when you were about three and Beck is looking at you with the protective air of a covetous older sister. I found the new picture in my wallet. It is only about two inches high and in it you are wrapped in a towel, standing with your legs apart on a beach. I'm not sure which beach. You are about seven so I think it is in Spain. Your hair is really long and a rich rust colour. It looks as if it has been having a fight with itself. Knotted strands criss-cross your face. Your legs, what I can see of them, and your shoulders are nut brown. You are a little Red Indian.

Last week, before I started writing to you again, I forgot to take the pills for a few days. I couldn't stop crying. I didn't want to cry. I literally couldn't stop. The tears, the need to let go, was ever present. I was really irritable, on edge, and I kept misjudging things. I broke two glasses and in the car I found myself consumed by road rage, cursing other drivers for the slightest indiscretion.

Horsey began to annoy me with his constant talking and his insane need to tell me, word for word, the entire story of the last episode of *Sponge Bob Squarepants*. I am convinced that he may be slightly autistic. If I ask him about school, depending on his mood, he will recount in real time every detail of a particular lesson. Recently in maths Billy was given a detention for repeatedly dropping his pencil. Horsey was appalled. 'All he did was drop his pencil,' he squawked. When he gets excited, Horsey sounds like a crow being pulled backwards through a small hole in a fence.

Anyway I've been taking the pills again for at least a week and I think that they do dull the pain. They act like a sponge. They soak up the tears and they soak up memories. There is no physical difference. I still have energy, not much but some. I am not a zombie. I think about you all the time but I can't bring you to life.

I will ask the doctor tomorrow what he thinks about the pills.

Goodnight, my angel. I love you so much.

Daddy

Hello, poppet,

It is 6/6/06: the date Robbie has been waiting for. The number of the beast. The day the world ends. It is half past ten at night so there is still time. I shall not mind if it means I will see you again.

I'm sorry I didn't write yesterday. I went to the doctor in the morning. Later I mowed the lawn because Horsey wanted to play cricket and he complains if the surface isn't flat enough. I paid some more bills with Mummy's credit card. It is the only one left with any credit to spare. In the afternoon I went to see Oma.

Doctor Tayler and I have become friends of sorts. I've always thought that being friends with your doctor is rather like being friends with your bank manager or the local police constable: probably advisable but not above suspicion. I sat in the waiting room, vaguely aware of the loudspeaker periodically calling for a Mr Bloggs or a Mrs Shipton. I had barely turned to page two of *The Reader's Digest Medical Dictionary* when Doctor Tayler appeared in person. 'Reg,' he said, 'how good to see you.' And then he put his arm around my shoulders and led me away. I felt twenty pairs of eyes boring into my back. 'There he goes,' I heard them thinking. 'He either has a terminal disease or he owes the doctor money.'

I told the doctor that I am worried about the pills. Sometimes I can't find you. It is as if a door has closed and you are behind it and I can't open it. I know you are there but it is not a door any more. It is an abyss, a gulf, and it is getting wider. You are standing on the other side and all the time you are getting smaller and further away so that I can't see you except for an outline, a shape growing indistinct in the distance. I fill in your features from memory but then I start to question the shape of your nose, the curve of your lips, and the harder I try to remember, the more impossible it becomes to bring you back until I find myself staring at the wall with only your name and a head full of straw. I can look at your picture of course but I need you with me all the time. I was wrong when I said the pills don't dull the pain. They do but I think that maybe dull pain is worse.

The doctor decided to halve the strength of the pills, from 10mg to 5mg. Then he checked my blood pressure, which is very high. I was not in the least surprised. How could it not be high? He is going to check it again next Monday and if it hasn't dropped, then I will have some more pills to add to my unpronounceable anxiety suppressants. I have made an appointment for Mummy to see Doctor Tayler on Friday. As I got up to leave I asked him whether he thought forty-eight was too old to have another baby. He said no but there is a one in fifty chance that the child could have Down's syndrome.

I was terrified even mentioning the idea of a baby to

the doctor and on the odd occasion that Mummy and I have talked about the possibility, I have been unable to leave unsaid the terrible thought that trying to have another baby might in some way be an attempt to replace you. Nothing could replace you. I said the same to the doctor. I am ashamed of the thought but others may think it and I feel compelled to scream that you are irreplaceable. Regardless of what Doctor Tayler said, we may be too old anyway.

I haven't done much work for David Rozalla lately. A pile of your grandfather's books lie unscanned next to my desk. After the publication of the RSSB report we were besieged by journalists, not just from the local papers but from the BBC and Channel 4. A film crew from the BBC came to the house to interview me. I hate the idea of being on television but we need all the publicity we can get to keep up the pressure on Network Rail. The night before, I read the report again and made five pages of notes, enough to speak continuously for about half an hour. When the crew arrived they told me that I was to be part of a three minute-slot on *BBC Look East* that same evening. I didn't watch myself but apparently I got to say one line, something about the Highway Code that had slipped out and made little sense when I said it and even less on TV.

I was given another chance the next day by Channel 4 *News at Noon*. They rang at nine in the morning and asked whether I could be at the studios by 11 a.m. I said that I would try. I gathered up my notes from the previous day and set off. Mummy came with me and on the way she tried to calm me down and made me run through what I wanted to say. Halfway there I had an idea. I would challenge Network Rail. If they say that building a bridge is too expensive, then we will find a way to build one ourselves. We could set up a charity and go to local businesses and to the BAA at Stansted Airport.

We arrived outside the Channel 4 News building at one minute to eleven. A parking ticket and a failed congestion charge payment notwithstanding, the interview was a success. We were met at reception and led to the studio by a strange robotic young woman who had escaped from an early episode of *Doctor Who*. She had obviously been brainwashed by the Cybermen but at least she knew the way. Neither Mummy nor I had ever been in a television studio before. The ceiling was racked with hundreds of spotlights and the entire far wall was a blue screen. A solitary, unremarkable desk stood in the middle of the floor surrounded by three television cameras mounted on what appeared to be industrial floor cleaners. A very tall man in a dark suit with hair like a *Thunderbirds* puppet was standing next to the desk. A blonde girl wearing Batman's utility belt came to meet us. She said that the whole thing would be over in fifteen minutes and asked me whether I wanted to go into 'make-up'. I can hear your hoots of laughter echoing inside my head. I politely declined.

The newsreader's name was Alex Thomson, a kind of coincidence in itself, but very soon he told me that he lived locally and often used Elsenham station to get to work. As we were talking, I saw Mummy out of the corner of my eye suddenly embrace the girl with the Bat belt. She then ran over to me and told me that her name was Pauline Gill, the daughter of Jean Gill, the lovely Scottish lady who has done what passes for my books for the last ten years. She still lives at home with her mother and father in Bishop's Stortford. Jean Gill came to your service and I had spoken to her only the day before. I found the whole thing too weird, an extraordinary combination of coincidences. I said my piece and threw down the gauntlet to Network Rail. Channel 4 broadcast every word.

When we got home Mummy and I told everybody, the Wiggetts, Paul and Mel, Oma, Uncle Davy and Auntie Trish, John and Murray. We even went round to see Andy and Mel Nimmo and stood in their kitchen and drank a bottle of wine. They all thought that you had stage-managed the whole thing. Sometimes I believe it. Sometimes life seems too strange for it not to be true.

The next day I received a phone call in the afternoon. 'This is Alex Thomson,' said the voice, 'Channel 4 News.'

'Ah, Mr Thomson,' I said.

'Call me Alex,' said the voice and then, after only the faintest pause, 'We interviewed an executive from Network Rail today. I thought you'd like to know. They say that if you want to build a bridge, you can go ahead and build one. As I said, I thought you'd like to know.'

So we have a purpose. Already we have found out enough to know that the whole project will be fraught with complications and indeed, it may not even be possible. Yvonne McPartland has arranged for a structural engineer to visit the station to carry out a feasibility study. We are awaiting the results. In the meantime all we can do is plan and hope.

Livvy's father, Chris Bazlinton, carries on his one-man crusade. He has persuaded one of the local papers to run a campaign with an on-line petition calling for Network Rail to LOCK THE GATES. I have great admiration for him but I find him a bit unapproachable. Our shared grief has not brought us together. A few weeks ago the local paper called and asked whether I would mind meeting a reporter at the station for a photograph to support the campaign. When I arrived, Chris was there with his other daughter, Stevie. Stevie was lovely, shy but warm but with Chris I felt like the office junior. We had to stand next to the gate through which you and Livvy had walked. I found myself hunched and terrified, barely able to think or speak. At regular intervals trains hurtled by within a few feet of us. They are no longer trains to me but creatures from nightmares and from my waking dreams. I do not know how I will go back there again or whether I ever can.

I love you, sweetheart. You are never out of my thoughts and I will never stop searching for you.

Your Daddy

Poppet,

Two days have passed. The sun continues to shine from a cloudless, pale blue sky. Mummy hasn't been to school this week. A pall of sadness has descended upon her. I feel it too. A subtle change in the nature of our grief.

I was in Saffron Walden yesterday at lunchtime. I had to go to the bank and to buy some chocolates for one of our increasingly rare hamper orders. I turned the corner at the bottom of the high street next to the ABC Barbecue. What amounted to a small horde of schoolgirls, all laughing and giggling and completely oblivious to the world, forced me into the road. Every one had your face, your hair. I could see your bare legs, the way your skirt moved with every step. You were laughing, your cheeks flushed red and your hair tangled and wild. They were your age, probably year nine. After they had passed, I felt drained. The shock of knowing that I will never see you again is almost too much to bear.

Auntie Trish called and begged us to go over to Southfork this weekend. She said that Uncle Davy had cleaned the pool and we could swim and eat outside on the patio. I didn't have to ask Mummy. I just said that we couldn't. I know Auntie Trish needs us as we need her and she knows she is always welcome here but we cannot go there. To swim without you, to eat without your endless chatter, to be able to leave without you begging us to stay for just a little bit longer, another half an hour. It's not possible, not yet anyway.

For such a long time I have been comforted or maybe protected by good memories. I was going to say 'happy' but it doesn't seem to be the right word. Now, more and more, I see you in pain or at those moments of your greatest distress. Taking you to school last year, seeing you in the driving mirror sitting in the back, your face drawn in pain. Even now I can see the huge tears gathering in the corners of your eyes. You would wait until Robbie and Horsey had got out of the car and then you would plead with me to take you home. 'Please, Daddy, please can I go home. It hurts so much.' Your voice stricken with pain and desperation. And sometimes I would relent and tell you to keep your head down so that none of the teachers would see you but, thinking back, I can't see why it would have mattered. You were in pain and not able to go to school. If I was in a good mood or not too tense or late for work, I would reach over and hold your hand as we drove home. I can feel your hand in mine now as I type, so hot, your grip so fierce. I knew why you were in pain but I never mentioned it to you. Mummy had said to me how rotten she thought it was that you had started so young. But that is the way of things now. We all grow up too quickly. But there had been times when I made you get out of the car because I thought that all your friends would probably be suffering

284

in the same way and that if they could go to school, then so could you. And I drove off watching you, your head down, walking so slowly. How could I have done that? How could I have been so cruel? I can't bear to go on. I will write again later. I love you so much.

My angel,

I couldn't go back to the computer on Friday and it is
now Sunday lunchtime. It is incredibly hot, nearly 30
degrees, and we are all sweating with our tempers barely
held in check. Robbie has completed half of his GSCEs
and should be revising but I can hear him in the living
room, strumming his guitar.

Yesterday afternoon we had another vicious row. I had
just watched the football on my own. The World Cup has
started and it was England's first match. Mummy was
sunbathing in the garden and Horsey had gone to play
with Di Nicholson's son in Debden Green. Robbie and
Cheese were upstairs in Robbie's bedroom, possibly
revising. The house was silent but for the drone of the
television and the moronic babble of the commentators.
I felt unutterably alone. Your absence sucks me in like a
black hole and I cannot rid myself of desperate memories.
As the match drew to a close, Robbie burst into the
room, his face deathly white and his eyes black with anger
or grief or both.

'When are you going to take me to Newport?' he
demanded, as if I had been keeping him waiting for hours
and his patience had finally run out.

'Don't talk to me like that,' I said. 'I'm not a dog or your servant.'

There was a moment of electric silence as if a huge black cloud hovered between us and was deciding whether or not to unleash its fury on the world. Then Robbie said that he was sorry, albeit through clenched teeth. I let it pass, accepted his apology and asked him whether he needed any money. He said no meaning yes and I dug in my pocket and found £4, which I held out towards him. 'I suppose I can borrow some more,' he said.

That was when I snapped. I give him money every day and no matter how much, he manages to spend it all. I don't know how our doors survive the periodic slamming. According to Andy they are the cheapest doors you can buy, £17 each from Homebase. I know they are hollow and I am sure I could put my fist through one if I really put my mind to it. I went through one door, Robbie went through the other and, with almost perfect coordination, we slammed each door so hard that the whole house shook. I went to sit in the utility room with the cat bowls and the dirty washing, desperate to be alone and not to let the others see my tears.

After a while I made my way sheepishly back into the kitchen. Mummy was standing by the sink and Robbie was in the corner by the microwave. Both had been crying. As I came in Robbie left. He wouldn't look at me. Mummy turned towards me. She had stopped crying but there was a look close to panic in her eyes. 'I'm not taking sides,' she said, 'but Robbie's only sixteen. He thinks he's close to cracking up. You're the one who's got to be strong.'

I found Robbie in the study, curled up in the corner of the fold-out settee. He was covering his face with his hands and I could see that he was crying even though he was not making a sound. I knelt on the floor in front of him and tried to hug him and he didn't push me away. I said that I was sorry and he said that he was sorry too. I love him so much. I love Horsey so much. Maybe I am demanding too much from them, in some way trying to bleed even more affection out of them to compensate for the terrible void that your absence has created. After about half an hour Robbie seemed OK again. I drove him to Newport where he spent the evening with Chitson and Cheese and Charlie McP. I picked him up at midnight and he seemed relaxed. Mummy and I barely spoke throughout the evening and Horsey, having returned from the Nicholsons' where he had been forced to eat salami, broccoli and tuna fish salad, the three things he hates most in the world, watched a film called *The Rock* with Sean Connery.

I've been meaning to tell you but I keep forgetting. We saw Paul and Mel again on Friday. We met in the Fleur de Lys in Widdington and sat in the garden and drank cider. The last time we went there was with you nearly a year ago. You had sat on the fence with Beck, making faces at car drivers as they passed and talking about the things that you talked about, things that I would never have guessed and seldom tried to imagine. Paul and Mel tried to distract us but each time that we do something again for the first time, it is impossible to escape being drawn down into the well of memories. And I don't want to escape.

The sun must have gone to Mel's head because she started telling us about the time when she and Paul had met. Paul had been so thin that he could easily wear her jeans and she had tested them for tightness on the basis that if she couldn't get her hands between the waistband and Paul's stomach, then they were too tight. Mummy and I were shocked. Mel is somebody who regards skirts that are above midcalf length to be too revealing. Paul said that he had never been that thin and that she must have been thinking of somebody else. He was sensibly wearing dark glasses and looked like a burly stand-in for Pierce Brosnan in a James Bond film.

They are going on holiday at the beginning of July, to the South of France, near Carcassonne. With perfect timing they will be away during the very week when we most probably have to move. I was relying on Paul to dismantle the dishwasher and the washing machine but now I shall have to do it myself. Alan Wiggett has already refused to help, saying that he is much better at organising. He says that if we can set up a video link to his laptop computer, he will advise us from the comfort of his own garden. Most of Robbie's friends have offered to help, however. Chitson, Cheese, Calvert, Joe, Gary, little Matt, Spuggy, Lou, Charlie McP and Sam. All they are asking for is a crate of beer.

Now that the move is imminent, both Mummy and I are dreading it. We will have to pack everything up and with the exploration of a cupboard or a chest of drawers or of a myriad different boxes and plastic bags strewn about the house, we will find more memories of you. More reminders that we will be moving without you and leaving behind the last house where we were all together and happy with days filled with laughter as well as tears.

There is something else that I need to tell you. We are going on holiday ourselves. Yvonne and Peter McPartland, Charlie McP's parents, have invited us to join them at their cottage in the Dordogne. We will only have to pay for our air fares We are going for a week at the beginning of August. They e-mailed us a picture of their house. It is a simple bungalow, painted white, and the front door is lost in a jungle of what might be wild roses. Wooded hills surround it on three sides and to the front it overlooks a medieval French village, half of the houses seemingly cut out of the rocks in the hillsides. A wild river thunders out of the centre of the village and under a spectacular Roman viaduct. If life were normal, if we were all together, I know that both Mummy and I would be counting down the days. You would already have begun packing your case, selecting which shampoos to take, which suntan lotions, headbands, jewellery, swimming costumes. Every Saturday afternoon between now and take-off would be spent in Cambridge, searching for just the right beach shoes, shorts and tops. But since we booked the tickets Mummy and I haven't talked about the holiday. Horsey needs a passport but neither of us has filled out the form, which even now is lying on my desk in plain sight. We will go, I know we will, but I don't want to and without asking I know Mummy doesn't want to go either.

I love you so much. The strain of not having seen you for so long and knowing that I will never see you again is becoming intolerable.

Bless you.

Daddy

13 June 2006

Hello, darling,

It is Tuesday evening. Robbie did his maths GCSE today and soon I will have to pick him up from Newport. He has chemistry tomorrow, then physics and history on Thursday and finally business studies on Friday. He has been revising at Cheese's house. She has been wonderful. She is naturally academic and her desire to do well has rubbed off on Robbie. I have heard them testing each other and arguing over the meaning of photosynthesis and strange, meaningless algebraic formulas.

For the second week running Mummy has been unable to go back to school. She says that she may never be able to go again. I have not talked to her about it or put pressure on her in any way. Maybe she will wake up one morning and the need or the desire will have returned. Now she seems to have disappeared within herself. She spends hours on the computer, playing cards, or searching on eBay for dresses to wear to Auntie Jill's wedding. The book she has been reading lies unfinished in the bathroom. She hasn't read a page in weeks. We had seemed to be climbing slowly out of the darkness but we have both fallen back, Mummy perhaps more so than me.

Auntie Jill calls and e-mails with a constant stream of

ideas to do with the wedding reception and suggestions
about what to wear. Mummy can only see what might
have been. Your first wedding. Your first opportunity to
be a bridesmaid. You would have gone shopping together
for dresses, spent hours, if not days, leafing through
catalogues. The whole summer would have been a
glorious build-up to the big day. For Mummy, much
more so than for me, it is a dagger through the heart. Not
only will you never be a bridesmaid, you will never be a
bride. I found Mummy in the kitchen two days ago
holding your picture. Under her breath she was saying
over and over again, 'the most beautiful girl who ever
lived'.

As I type I understand better why I am struggling so
desperately just to get through each day. Summer is
upon us. Horsey is busy working out to the nearest
minute exactly how long he has left before he breaks up
for the holidays. Sports day is less than a month away.
Our neighbours have already christened their new
barbecue, the acrid smell of firelighters and paraffin
mingled with that of burnt sausages and undercooked
chicken wafting over the garden fence. We don't have a
barbecue although doubtless you would have forced me
to buy one by now. At the first hint of a hot day you
would have dragged me into the garage to find last
year's paddling pool and stood over me as I blew it up,
the exertion finally resulting in burst blood vessels in
both my eyes. I asked Horsey at the weekend whether
he wanted me to get the pool out but he said he wasn't
bothered. I don't think he's very keen on sitting in it on

his own. Anyway it was only ever an excuse to have a series of increasingly violent water fights at the end of which everybody would be in tears and you would walk through the house dripping wet, leaving a trail of sodden footmarks all across the living-room carpet and through the rest of the house to your bedroom door. You would appear in the kitchen a little later wearing at least three towels, one wrapped like a turban around your head, one around your shoulders and one tied around your waist, whereupon you would hurl yourself down on the settee and demand food.

We haven't been to the sea this year. Last year we had already been to Aldeburgh by now and to Wells in Norfolk. You were the only one brave enough to walk across Aldeburgh beach without shoes, two miles of assorted pebbles, flints and razor-sharp shells with not a single speck of sand to be seen. You don't often see people swimming at Aldeburgh, especially not at the beginning of June, but nothing ever stopped you. You had your bathing suit on under your clothes, which you discarded at random on your way down to the sea. 'Come on, Daddy,' you said, 'I'm not going in without you,' which was OK because like you, when I see the sea I just have to go in. Mummy didn't mind because she had seen it all before, except she tried to look away when I took my shirt off and she moved further down the beach so that people wouldn't think she was with us. Horsey and Robbie threw stones at each other and at seagulls, and steadfastly refused even to take off their shoes. We went in. I can feel the cold now, icy clamps around my ankles. I can hear you laughing too, falling backwards into the surf and pulling me after you. The shock was appalling. I immediately ran back up on to the beach, lacerating my feet on the grisly array of deadly stones in the process. And all I could hear was your evil cackle booming from the breakers, 'What's the matter, Fatty, too cold for you?'

Oma used to get so annoyed when you insulted me in public, which you did very often and very loudly. When Oma was with us I would pretend to be angry and admonish you mildly with a stern 'You really should respect your father, Charlie,' in response to which you would hoot with laughter and stare at me with your eyes bulging and your mouth as wide open as possible. Privately I loved the way you would insult me. It was a game to you, to see how far you could push me and what you could get away with. You reserved your most stinging put-downs for those you most loved. I knew that.

I was sitting on the settee last night, next to Horsey watching something or other, I can't remember what. Horsey, taken by a moment of painful honesty, observed that the excess flesh around my elbows was 'disgusting'. I had forgotten how you would knead the loose skin, often when you were very tired and on the verge of sleep. I loved the feeling as you rolled the flesh between your fingers and then, as sleep started to take you, your hand would climb blindly up my arm to the shoulder and then across to my neck, searching for my ear lobe. Your touch was so delicate, so intimate. I cannot believe that I have not thought of it until this moment and now I can think of nothing else.

So much has gone. So much has been taken away. I will dream of you.

I love you.

Daddy

17 June 2006

Sweetheart,

Four days have passed. It is Saturday and the turgid heat
has returned, sapping our strength and leaving us lethargic
and without the desire to do anything.

We can no longer rent the house in Newport that I
told you about. The people who live there have decided
not to move. That is their right, it is still their house.
Since Wednesday we have looked at three other
possibilities. One is too small, only one room downstairs
with a kitchen the size of an airing cupboard. It is has the
advantage of being cheap but I do not know where I
would work and there is nowhere for us to escape from
each other if the need arises. Another was too big and too
grand, the hall and galleried landing alone big enough to
convert into a one-bedroomed apartment. The people
who live there now are young and obviously successful
with two tiny children. We walked around their home
saying all the right things and nodding in the right places.
Mummy stood in the daughter's bedroom staring silently
at the cot and all the assembled paraphernalia of a life
beginning. We left and sat in the car where Mummy
broke down, the need to howl out loud for once not
suppressed. I tried to cuddle her and she spoke between

297

waves of shuddering sobs. 'We used to be like that once,' she said.

We looked at another house yesterday. It is too expensive but we have less than a week before we exchange contracts and we have to live somewhere. We will have money over from the sale and Rob Loe at the County High has asked me to do some more lectures. Maybe fate has in store for me to become a teacher. There are worse things to be.

Robbie finished his exams. He went camping last night with Joe, Cheese and Chitson in Joe's two-man tent, which is barely big enough for Chitson on his own, let alone all four of them. He rang about an hour ago to say they were all right and could they go into Stansted and would I pick them up around 5 p.m.

It is Father's Day tomorrow. I didn't know until Horsey told me that I would be taking him to the cinema to celebrate. I was never very good at Father's Day to begin with. I think I inherited from Oma the idea that every day should be Father's Day and it is just an excuse for card shops to make lots of money. You loved it though, just as you loved Mother's Day and every other day that, for even the slightest reason, justified a party or an excuse for you to do the cooking. Last year you brought me breakfast in bed and a card, and then you made it your duty to prevent anybody from asking me to do anything that you thought I might not want to do, like play Monopoly with Horsey or spend half the day ferrying Robbie back and forth. I wasn't, however, excluded from doing what you wanted me to do, which included going for a bike ride and watching a series of unspeakable programmes like *America's Top Model*, *Big Brother*, *Charmed* and anything else that wasn't *The Simpsons*.

I went into the utility room to feed the cats this morning. I had to move a black bin liner full of washing and underneath it was a drawer full of cards and old bills. The card on the top was the card you got for me last year. I picked it up and read it. This is what you wrote:

Hello, Daddy,

    I know we've been through hard times lately and dealed with things most families don't have to deal with. I want you to know that everything will be OK because our family shares so much love. That is all we need. As long as we have each other anything is possible. As long as I am with my family I can go through anything and come out the other side with just as much love for you as I did when I went in. I love you Daddy more than an infinity of giant buffalos charging.

    You are my daddy and the best Daddy in the world at that. I will love you forever and nothing can change that. Nothing will change that!

    I love you Pupps.

    Me XXX

That is what you wrote. You used to call me 'Pupps'. I've got to stop now. I am crying and Mummy has come to see if I am OK. She is crying too. How can you have written that and it not be true? How can you not be here?

It's half past six. The afternoon has gone by and I went shopping. Robbie rang to ask for more time so I have taken my shoes off. He will have to wait for me now.

Mummy said to me that only the knowledge that she saw you yesterday and that she will see you again tomorrow gives her the strength to get up in the morning and somehow negotiate her way through each day. What remains of this life is today.

Poppet,

I'm sorry I just stopped writing before. I am almost paralysed with sadness. Yesterday was Father's Day. It was also exactly a year to the day since we went to see Green Day at Milton Keynes.

I bought the papers as I always do on a Sunday and positioned myself at the kitchen table with a cup of tea and a cigarette. I arranged your photographs in a semi circle so that I could see you from every angle. Like a moth to a lighted candle, I found myself drawn to the same hideous articles. I was particularly impressed by one entitled 'Seven Steps to Buying the Perfect Trainers'. I need some new shoes. I have been wearing the pair that Uncle Stu left here last summer for at least three months. You will remember them. You tried to throw them away because they have a seam that runs down the centre as if they had been stitched together by a blind person. A passing fashion, in fact a fashion passing so fast that only Stu was quick enough to buy a pair. I went into Clarks in Saffron Walden with the intention of purchasing something more appropriate but when it came to it, I just couldn't muster up the enthusiasm to make a choice. Who cares? I thought, and walked out. That's how I feel about almost everything now. I don't feel it about writing to you. I have to write to you. When I write to you, you are the centre of my world and I can think of nothing else but you. Sometimes I can't think of anything to say but just sitting here in front of the computer screen is better than doing anything else. Telling you the smallest thing, keeping you a part of all our lives.

Auntie Trish calls me at least twice a week. I rarely see her at the moment because she is working in the kitchen at Reggiano's making the sandwiches. So I talk to Trish on the telephone and we try to comfort each other. If she calls on a Saturday she will say she knows that it is worse for me than on any other day of the week because your accident was on a Saturday and although I don't show it I get quite annoyed. Why should it be worse on a Saturday? It is intolerable every day. It's the same as when people found out about the accident and some said to us, 'Oh, I'm so sorry and it must be so much worse at Christmas.' I know people don't really know what they are saying but sometimes I can't stand it. How could anything be any worse on any day than losing you? And yet, somehow, yesterday was worse. Mummy and I barely exchanged two words. There was no anger, no argument. Sometimes we just look at each other and there is still nothing to say. Nothing that either of us can think of that might comfort the other. Horsey has found a new book and wouldn't be parted from it until it was time to go to the cinema at 4 p.m. Robbie slept all day, recovering from his camping experience. I asked Mummy whether she wanted to come to the cinema but she just shook her head. Robbie came and fell asleep having been awake for only about an hour and half.

Every film I see, every book I read seems to be about a father desperately trying to save his daughter. In the film a girl is trapped on a sinking ship and eventually her father, having tried everything he can to save her, sacrifices his own life so that she might live. I watched in a kind of trance. I wasn't even given the chance to try to save you. I said goodbye to you in the morning. I kissed your forehead as you lay in bed and stroked your hair. I didn't give it a second thought. I knew that I would see you again in a few hours. In the book I am reading, which I thought was about something else, a father spends his life searching for his daughter. He gives up his job, his money, his house, his self-respect. I can't do anything. I wasn't even allowed to see you afterwards.

I have been thinking about God or whatever God might be. In the papers, in between the articles about training shoes and which is the best beach to party on and this summer's must-have barbecues and endless pictures of footballers' wives trying to take too much luggage through customs, there are stories of quiet misery. This weekend a whole family was killed in a car accident in the Lake District. A man, his wife and three children. Every day forty or twenty or sixty people are killed in Iraq. The endless killing has become so commonplace that each story appears on the news as a kind of postscript, just after the human interest piece about the cunning fox who stole a baby's rattle right out of its cot and an amusing sketch involving the Deputy Prime Minister and a croquet mallet.

The daily toll of children dying from AIDS and starvation and malaria isn't even worth a mention.

I heard a woman talking on the radio whose daughter had been murdered. Although her daughter had been killed almost five years ago, she sounded empty as if all hope had been scoured away. She said that she had always thought that the worst thing that could happen to any parent was to lose a child but now she knew that there was something worse. I listened to her and I felt ashamed. I know you were happy. You brought such happiness to others. With a simple sentence or just a smile you blessed the people you met. I try to tell myself that I am still lucky. Lucky to have been your father. To always be your father. To have been picked by fate or God or something beyond our understanding. I don't say this to Mummy but I hope that there are times when she feels the same.

So I think about God. On the day after the accident a priest came to see us, not the Reverend Titford, a different priest. A nice man with the best intentions but trapped by his beliefs. In the midst of our shock and horror, Mummy asked him whether he believed that you were in heaven. He looked straight at Mummy and asked whether you had believed that Jesus died on the cross for our sins. What could Mummy say? The priest said that he couldn't say whether you were in heaven if you hadn't believed. I don't believe in the priest's God. I don't believe in a God who makes choices. Could I believe in God if he had spared you and taken someone else's daughter? I have tried to learn about Buddhism and I would dearly love to be a Buddhist but I can't just be one. But at the same time I look around me, I look at a world without faith, and I hate it. I've got to believe in something. I've got to believe in you, that some part of you, that the essence of you, lives on in some way that I can't understand.

To live a life without faith is like being the managing director of a huge company. You have to take responsibility for everything, all the time, and you can never have a day off, or even a minute. Some people might say that is a good thing but I think it breeds fear and selfishness and ultimately, hopelessness. Because if it is true that there is nothing, no design, no purpose, then every person who has ever lived, every animal, just blinks into existence strapped into a rollercoaster, spends a minuscule amount of time being flung up and down, and then blinks out of existence. I don't believe that's true and I don't see any point in believing it.

I've got to go and get Robbie in a minute and then it will be too late and I will be too tired. I've got to give another lecture on Wednesday to a group of student teachers. I can't help laughing because I have been told that I don't have the right qualifications to study to be a teacher without taking another degree but I am well enough qualified to teach the student teachers.

I love you. I long for you. I will keep writing, I promise.

Sleep well.

Your Daddy

My darling,

It is early on Wednesday evening. The sun is still shining but banks of thunderous-looking clouds are massing in the distance. I think there may be a storm later. Horsey is watching television and Mummy is in the bath. Robbie is with Cheese in Newport. Although he has finished his exams, Cheese still has one to do and Robbie has gone to lend her his support or to distract her and force her to go and play on the whirlybird swings down at the rec.

I gave my last lecture at about two o'clock at the County High. Actually it wasn't really a lecture. I had to judge a series of short films that the students have made over the past week and offer them the benefit of my so-called expertise. The County High has its own cinema, which is extraordinary. I have never heard of a school that has its own cinema. It's in the sports hall, which on any other day looks exactly like a sports hall. It has a polished wooden floor covered in a confusion of painted lines in a variety of garish colours, with ropes and climbing frames all over the place. At the touch of a button the far wall reveals itself to be a sort of giant, cantilevered seating system. When it is fully extended there are over 200 seats from the back row, which is near the ceiling, to the front row, which is at floor level. The opposite wall converts into a state-of-the-art projection screen and there is even a projection room. The only disappointment for me was a lack of anywhere obvious to buy hotdogs and popcorn.

The first film was called *Nestra,* which was a drawback because I didn't know what Nestra meant and the students didn't bother to tell me. Pretty soon I got the idea. The film was about a mother and father whose child had died, although whether Nestra was the name of the child or some obscure reference to Greek mythology, I never found out. With all the lights out and the blinds drawn over the windows, it was almost completely dark. The film was seven minutes long. I watched as one of the students, obviously cast as the mother, tossed and turned in her bed, troubled by some terrible nightmare as the camera cut to shots of an empty cot, a teddy bear face down on the carpet, a train set unused, its locomotive destined never to leave the station.

I watched the film and I watched myself. It's hard to explain. I am becoming two people. The real me, the one that I have to keep at home, hidden from the outside world, wanted to scream and run out of the room. The other me was sitting in his seat, looking interested, smiling even, capable of standing up afterwards and talking sensibly about what he had seen without letting anyone know that he really knew about grief, what it's like to get up every morning without hope, to stand in the kitchen looking out at the garden with one's mind totally blank, trying to think but not being able to, to go shopping and forget what you went for, to listen to your wife crying in the night and know there is nothing you can do.

The other film was about a woman who murders her sister. All things considered I preferred it.

It's very strange how the mind works. I remember reading once that there are five different emotional stages following a terrible trauma. In the wrong order, I think they are anger, denial, depression, a kind of false hope and finally acceptance. It occurs to me that there may be even more than two of me, there might be three or even four. It seemed for a while, when Mummy went back to school and I was getting ready to start my series of lectures at the County High and Robbie's exams loomed menacingly before him, that there might be hope. Now Mummy has sunk back into an endless grey depression. She no longer wants to see our friends although she will not turn anybody away. Paul and Mel and the Wiggetts sense it too. They call religiously. I do not believe there could be better friends in the world. John hasn't been to see us for about a month but he still calls at least twice a week. I think they sense a change, a need for us to find our own way forward. Uncle Davy hasn't called on me to help him with the deliveries for at least two months. Auntie Trish calls and Oma has shifted her focus for the time being, bringing her guns to bear on Uncle Davy's businesses and what he needs to do to make them work or work better.

I sit on the settee reading and find myself staring at the pictures of you on the mantelpiece and lined up across the top of the piano. There always seems to be a new one. There are some of you when you were a baby and one

taken when you were at Henham School wearing a
Victorian chambermaid's outfit that Mummy made for you
out of one of Robbie's old shirts. You are wearing a
white bonnet and you have your hair in pigtails. I can
remember the day. I can see you getting on the bus to
take you to Kentwell Hall in Long Melford and I can see
myself standing on the pavement outside the school gates
waving to you as the bus pulled away.

There is another where you are cheek to cheek with
Lou, Cheese's friend, at the Battle of the Bands in
Newport. It was last September. Robbie's band was
playing and half the school was there to watch. Somebody
told me at the time that there were more than 300 kids in
the hall. Mummy and I stood at the back and you
disappeared with your friends to get as close to the stage as
possible. It must have been quite cold because I can see
you wearing your green sweatshirt and blue jeans.
Mummy began to worry that you would be crushed at
the front and sent me to check on you. The band was
already playing and the noise was deafening. Everybody
was dancing and shouting, and some of the boys, probably
Chitson and Fleetwood, had started a mosh pit. I made
my way down the side of the hall to a point where I
could look across the stage to see where you were. I saw
you immediately. You had your back to me and you and
Lou were holding a home made poster and on it was
written in very large, unmistakable letters: 'MIKEY G, I'M
PREGNANT AND IT'S YOURS'. I'm still not entirely sure who
Mikey G is but you must have sensed me looking at you
because you turned and saw me and although you were

already as red as the world's reddest tomato, you went even redder and started pointing furiously at Lou.

After the last song Charlie McP took his shoes off and threw them into the crowd, the gesture of a true rock star in the making, except that he ruined it by asking for them back a few minutes later.

I have to remember everything. I go back over every holiday, trying to recall each moment, putting the days and the times in order. All the houses that we lived in. All the different places we went to. I've got thirteen years and I don't want to forget one second. Mummy has a locket of your hair in her jewellery box, which she keeps in the chest of drawers in our bedroom. I haven't looked at it but I know it is there.

It's very late now. Robbie rang earlier to ask whether he could stay at Cheese's house. Horsey is asleep and Mummy is waiting in the kitchen for her turn on the computer.

I know you know I love you.

Sleep well.

Daddy

Hello, my Charlikins,

Thursday afternoon. Another day is limping by. I received the contracts concerning the sale of the house in the post this morning. Once they have been signed and returned, then the deed is done and we will be on our way again. We will not go without you. The new house has four bedrooms and one will be yours. We are taking your bed and all your clothes and your posters, and we will put them up as best we can, hopefully in the way that you would want them.

I cannot imagine what it is going to be like to move without your ceaseless energy and enthusiasm. We have less than two weeks and we have done nothing. You would already have packed everything in your room, all the books throughout the house would be sorted and labelled, and together we would be planning endless trips to the dump to get rid of the huge amounts of rubbish that our family has always managed to accumulate. I showed Peter McPartland the inside of the garage on Saturday when he came round to pick up Charlie McP. I do not get the impression that he is a man who is easily shocked but his eyes widened noticeably and there was a certain slackness around the jaw when he saw the mountain of dilapidated cardboard boxes, assorted bicycles and broken washing machines which, for some inexplicable reason, we have never been able to part with. If you're wondering why I showed him the inside of the garage, it's because he rashly suggested that his garage was messier than ours. He won't make the same mistake again.

We are going to see Paul and Mel tonight. The contract needs to be witnessed by non-family members who are trustworthy.

Oma has gone to see Auntie Franky in Rome. I drove her to the airport and she insisted that we arrive a minimum of two hours before take-off because that's what it said on the ticket. I hadn't realised that this is her first trip for two years, the two years of horror as she calls them. The last time she went to Italy, Dan was still alive and her greatest worry was my lack of a proper job. She feels that this may be her last journey. I don't say anything when she says this, I just listen. There is no place for platitudes or trite expressions of hope. She is eighty-three. Tiredness and despair have caught up with her. I look at her and although she is still remarkable for her age, I can no longer see the woman she used to be lurking beneath the surface. She seems smaller to me yet she retains tremendous pride in her appearance and in the way that she carries herself. We sat together and had a cup of tea but her hands shake so much that she can no longer safely transfer the liquid to her mouth without the fear of spilling it, and you know what Oma is like if she spills something on her clothes. I couldn't help her. She wouldn't allow it and to try would have embarrassed us both.

I know it is impossible but sometimes I try to imagine what it must be like to be her. She has lost two of her most beloved grandchildren, she has been alone for over thirty years and she is nearing the end of her life. Yet she still laughs, still plays bridge, still involves herself absolutely in the lives of her children whether they like it or not. At eighty-three she travels alone to Italy. What does she think about when she lies alone at night in her bed? What motivates her to go on?

I am terrified of the future. Terrified of growing old without you. I wonder, quite often, why I do not spend most of my time screaming out loud. I am drawn back again and again to the day of your accident. I lie awake in bed and I see you at the crossing with Livvy. I try to imagine what happened to you and I pray that your mind didn't even have time to take anything in before it was over. I don't understand why I don't start screaming. I don't understand why I am not screaming now. I don't understand how I can ever be normal and why I have not gone mad. And I realise it's because I don't believe it. It's not real. You are with me all the time. I see your face, your hair, your smile, whether I have my eyes open or closed. I can feel your lips as you kiss me on the cheek. I can hear your voice and I can see you as you sleep. I can feel the slow, steady pulse of your heart.

Maybe I am mad but I will never let you go, never.

My darling,

It is nearly midnight on Friday. Mummy is asleep. She
has been with Adele since this morning and I only went
to pick her up about an hour ago. Horsey stayed home
from school to help me pack, and Robbie is at the
Newport School ball or prom or whatever it is called. He
didn't want to go but for Cheese's sake he put on a brave
face and a pinstripe jacket and a black shirt with a red tie
that Mummy bought for him on eBay. He looked great,
like a rock star. You would be so proud of him.

On Monday I went to London to the headquarters of
Network Rail to hand over a petition demanding that they
lock the gates at Elsenham station. We collected over 3,000
signatures although most of the credit should go to Livvy's
dad and to the local paper. A reporter was there and a
photographer. Chris Bazlinton and I had to stand in the
reception of the Network Rail building and have our
pictures taken holding a box full of signed petition papers.
Two helpless and innocent middle managers from the
company's publicity department were sent down to meet
us. They looked terrified and exhausted, as if they hadn't
slept for a week. We shook hands with them and they said
how sorry they were and how appalling it must be for us.

I looked around. It was the biggest reception area I have ever been in, like an enormous, deserted platform, devoid of colour or life. Acres of uniform, grey tiles and grey walls, with no flowers or plants or paintings and nowhere to sit. Purgatory's waiting room. I wanted to cry. One of the men said that there would be a meeting to discuss possible safety improvements to the station. I said to them that I didn't understand why, after nearly seven months, absolutely nothing had been done. The gates remain unlocked. There is no 'fast train approaching' sign, no guard to warn people, no nothing. I said that I thought Network Rail must be hoping that the inquest finds them guiltless and that it will be decided that it was your fault because you were not an expert on the railway code. That way the company won't have to spend any money. The men looked embarrassed and stared at the grey-tiled floor. I was grateful to them for that, at least.

Later I had a drink with my old friend John Hayward whom you met once when I was at FilmFour. He has just left his job and at fifty-five he knows it won't be so easy to find another. I had forgotten that he had met you about four years ago when you had come to work with me at FilmFour and you had spent the day tormenting Jules and Karin and the other girls in the office. At lunchtime John took us to the bar of the Charlotte Street Hotel and we sat at a table near to the actress Cate Blanchett who smiled at you and made you blush even though you didn't know who she was.

Now that the GCSEs are over, Robbie and the band are practising again. They played live at Saffron Walden

Town Hall last night in the Battle of the Bands and came second. It is the first time that they haven't come last or been disqualified. Robbie said that they got the most audience votes but the judges gave first prize to some band called the Spores because Charlie McP threw a can of Red Bull into the crowd, which is against the rules and the sort of behaviour that is frowned upon in Saffron Walden. If Charlie McP could sing he would already be famous and going out with Kate Moss.

Today has been one of the worst days I can remember although I find it impossible to conceive of having a good day. We are moving on Tuesday and I have been clearing out the garage. I borrowed Uncle Davy's van and took the fridge, a washing machine and a rusty bicycle to the dump. I made a second journey with bags full of mouldy curtains and mildewed jackets, boxes of tired, broken toys and old strimmers. I even threw away two ancient computers, both of which I have owned since before you were born. I have never really been able to come to terms with the idea that computers are inherently valueless the minute you take them out of the case.

Having got rid of some of the bigger stuff, I was able to tackle the foothills of the box mountain. Each box I came to had your name written on it in pink felt tip. I opened each one, sitting in the dust on the garage floor. I found your Victorian dolls, stacked neatly in rows of three, all individually wrapped in tissue paper. One box contained all of your old exercise books from Henham School and your annual report cards. I read them all. I found a scrapbook you had made about yourself for your induction day at Newport. The cover was a collage of pictures all cut out and glued together with infinite care. One of you playing the violin; one of you holding the cat; two of Robyn Dane and Hannah Pallet, your best friends; a picture taken at Alton Towers of you on a rollercoaster, something terrifying called the Serpent's Claw or Dracula's Teeth, your hair streaming out behind you, your hands welded to the safety bar and your face exploding with joy. I sat on the garage floor and I started to cry and the more I cried, the harder it became to stop. Then I felt a hand on my shoulder. I turned and it was Sue the teacher who lives in the house on the corner. I got up and wiped the tears off my face and said I was sorry. I couldn't look her in the eye. She put her arm around me and told me that it was all right to cry.

Sue is retiring in nineteen days' time. She has been a teacher for thirty years. She had been looking forward to spending her retirement travelling with Angela, who lived in the house adjacent to us, which is nearly opposite but not quite, but Angela died two weeks ago. She was fifty-nine. Cancer. I remember somebody told us at Christmas that the cancer was in remission.

I dread the week ahead. There is so much to do. So many boxes to sort through, so many pictures, so many memories. Jill Wiggett and Yvonne McPartland are coming tomorrow to help Mummy to pack up your room.

I love you, poppet. I love you so much.

Bless you.

Daddy

Hello, my angel,

It feels as if I have been away but I no longer have a home to come back to. We are in the new house. I am sitting in my study which actually is a study and not a corner of the dining room or a space at the top of the stairs. My desk is next to the window, which looks out on the main road into Newport. Cars hurtle by remorselessly and planes take off overhead. In the garden we are sandwiched between the M11 and the mainline railway to Cambridge. We are never without noise. I find it quite comforting but maybe that is because my madness has passed the point of no return. As we are now renting again, we are subject to the rules and conditions of the owners. We are not allowed to smoke either inside or anywhere on the premises, nor are we allowed to keep pets, which is bad news for the cats who have officially ceased to exist. They still eat a lot though. There is a brisk new shed in the garden, which is supposed to be their new home.

It has taken since I last wrote to you to complete the move. Nearly two weeks. We have no garage here and the loft is full of pink fluff and not suitable for storing anything except for perhaps Elton John's wardrobe. I have

made about a hundred trips to the dump and thrown
away nearly everything we have ever owned. I have
thrown away nothing of yours, not on purpose anyway.
I am grateful to Mummy now for never letting me throw
away even one scrap of paper that you once doodled on.
I have found countless designs for the most exotic dresses
and hats. Hats in the shape of crocodiles and with whole
postboxes on the top. Hats with real plants growing
around the brim and one with a crescent moon complete
with a cow in mid-jump. I found stories and more poems
and once, sometime during last week, a letter that you
wrote to Mummy and me, saying how we had been so
mean to you and you wanted to leave home and how
horrible Horsey and Robbie were. I read it, disappearing
down a dark tunnel of misery.

I remembered what had happened. It was only last
September. Mummy had bought all three of you new
pencils and pens for the coming school term. You, of
course, lost all of your pencils almost immediately.
Sometime during the evening you asked Horsey whether
you could borrow one of his pencils. Naturally he said no,
adding in his own peculiarly pedantic way that if you had
already lost all your pencils, then it was your own fault
and that you should look after things better. I can hear
your screech of indignation quite clearly. 'So you don't
lose things then, Harry. Right, get real. I hate you Harry,
I hate you!'

I came to Horsey's defence. It seemed to me pretty
ridiculous that you had managed to lose all your pencils
without leaving either your room or the house in the

space of about two hours. What should have been a mild rebuke, a gentle word, turned into a hideous row. You called Mummy a witch and me a bastard, and said things to Horsey that I don't want to repeat, and then you stormed out of the house. I came to find you after a while. Eventually things were OK and I hope I cuddled you before you went to sleep.

And now I have found the letter. You wrote that Robbie and Horsey were always ganging up on you and being horrible to you and making you feel small, and that Mummy and I never listened to you, and that you loved us but you couldn't bear to live with us any more. I showed the letter to Mel. She had to tear it from my hands. I haven't shown it to Mummy.

Mel actually laughed. 'Typical teenage girl,' she said. 'You should see how many of these we've got from Beck.'

She wanted to make me feel better and in a way she did but I don't have any time left any more. I can't say I'm sorry. I can't make it better.

It was my birthday last week. I'm not going to lie and say I forgot but I didn't remind anybody. Mummy and Robbie and Horsey all forgot too which was good. So did Uncle Davy and Auntie Trish. Oma rang and said that she knew it was my birthday and that she was thinking of me. In the afternoon John Keeling rang and started singing 'Happy Birthday to you' down the phone for which I was grateful even though I wish he hadn't. The Wiggetts sent me a card and Paul and Mel e-mailed from France. I got one present, a book from Yvonne and Peter McPartland about the Cathars. The Cathars come or, more properly, came from the part of France that we are going to at the beginning of August, around Montpellier and Carcassonne in a region called Languedoc. They were most powerful at the beginning of the thirteenth century and unlike almost everybody else who has ever lived, they were Christians who practised tolerance and compassion. They didn't prejudge anybody on the basis of their colour or their beliefs. Not too surprisingly they were all but exterminated by order of the Pope by about 1250.

In the evening John drove all the way from Kelvedon to Newport to buy me a drink. We decided to walk to the pub which Robbie told us was just around the corner but actually turned out to be more than a mile away. Outside the pub there was a sign saying BEER GARDEN but it was more of a 'beer window box', a small, paved area wedged between the back wall of the toilets and a nine-foot-high fence, enough room for two modest tables and four chairs. We didn't have to fight for a seat. We drank three pints each and talked about Charles Darwin and the theory of evolution, which seems a bit pretentious, I admit, but I have just finished reading a book about Darwin and John loves highfalutin conversations in which he can show off his superior arguing abilities.

John put a question to me. If you were allowed to ask God one question, what would it be? I didn't want to ask God why you had to die. I know enough to know that nothing is personal. I'd been sitting with my head back, looking up at the stars. The longer I looked the more stars there seemed to be, barely discernible motes of light, lost in the glare of brighter, nearer stars. Why, I thought, if God made the universe, did he, she or it make everything so far away? As human beings, we can never even hope to travel to our nearest neighbour, a star called Alpha Centauri, which, according to John, is about four light years away. I'd like to believe that your soul or your spirit is free, travelling between the stars as easily as we might travel from Newport to Cambridge, and that death is just another evolutionary stage.

It was our wedding anniversary today. Twenty years. I think that may be some kind of precious stone, quartz or marble or something. Certainly better than wood. We both forgot anyway, at least until it was too late to do anything about it. I bought Mummy some flowers from the Spar and a bottle of wine.

I feel hollow, poppet, empty, and I look forward to nothing. At the end of July eight months will have passed but I no longer have a sense of time. Our life with you seems so long ago and so far away. You have become a star. I can see you but I can never reach you and I cannot bear it.

I love you.

Daddy

Hello, sweetheart,

I have let another two weeks pass without writing to you. I think of you all the time but this new house has had a strange effect on me. It is like living in a hugely disorganised hotel without room service and with no cupboards or wardrobes to hang anything up in. As we will have to move again in six months, Mummy and I have decided not to unpack, instead leaving boxes and black dustbin bags lining the walls of every room. We bought one large wardrobe from a second-hand furniture warehouse near Stansted airport but when the men came to deliver it, it was too wide to go up the stairs. So we went back and bought a smaller one that has enough room for some of Mummy's dresses and her growing collection of shoes, the result of her obsession with eBay. We are all sleeping upstairs now. There are no memories here. I know I will not see you at the top of the stairs or peering, hair bedraggled, from around the bathroom door. I am not frightened of the house or frightened of looking up and not seeing you. It is just a place to eat and sleep.

We are in the middle of a heatwave that shows no signs of slowing down, possibly for several years. I think the whole country has been towed to a different location, somewhere off the coast of India. We are all hot and sticky with no energy and no desire to do anything except sit outside and drink pints of orange juice. Even Paul Bowe has taken to wearing shorts in public, something that he swore he would never do. Mummy and I can't sit in the kitchen any more because there is no room for a table so we sit in the garden and read the papers and hold hands and think of you. It will be eight months at the end of July, 240 days.

Doctor Tayler rang on Friday, just to see how we are. I told him that I still feel that we are living in a dream but that life goes on, for the most part for us with a grim normality.

I spoke to Uncle Davy who says that he cannot understand why the world didn't stop when you and Dan were lost. He doesn't understand why the sun comes out and the shops stay open. He doesn't understand why the whole world isn't in mourning.

I read that more than 50,000 innocent civilians have died in Iraq since the end of the so-called war in 2003. Another tsunami struck the coast of Java last week, killing at least 600 people and leaving 75,000 homeless. Children are murdered every day. On the front page of one of the Sunday papers, there is a picture of a young woman with her two children. All three were killed when an Israeli bomb fell on their house in a country called the Lebanon. I tell you all this because I know that losing you doesn't make us special. I told Doctor Tayler that your death has helped me to understand true love. True love is giving your own life to save another. I wasn't given the chance to die instead of you but I know that I will never love you any less and that the intensity of my love for you will never diminish.

I didn't tell you before. A few weeks ago we received a letter from Mrs Greenhalgh, your old headteacher at Henham School. Several of the teachers led by Mrs Dunn, Jo Pallet and Kate Dane decided that they wanted to create an annual award in your honour. The award, to be known as the Charlie Thompson trophy, is for outstanding performance in creative writing and art. The trophy is so beautiful. It is made entirely of glass, a perfectly cut star on a tapering stem set on a heavy oblong base with your name engraved upon it. It is a million times more impressive than those glass slabs I used to win at FilmFour for designing the best video sleeve. We were asked to go on Friday to the year six leavers' assembly to present your trophy to its first winner. Mummy didn't want to go but she found the courage from somewhere. All the parents and teachers would be there, most of whom we still know but haven't seen since the accident.

We arrived early and hid in the staff room. Kate came to see us and said that we could stay out of sight until we were needed to hand over the trophy. The school is so familiar, every corridor, every room, echoing with memories of you. I could see you in your blue and white striped school dress, your socks around your ankles and your hair held precariously in a half falling to bits ponytail, whispering to Robyn and Hannah and pointing at Mrs Dunn behind her back; holding the hand of a tiny, ginger-haired year one pupil and guiding him gently back into his classroom; being told to stop running by Mrs Thomas.

Before we went in I stood by the gate next to the privet hedge staring at the playing fields, images of sports days washing over me. I always thought that it was unfair that they put you, Robbie and Horsey in Red House, which has come last since the school was built and will doubtless come last until the sun explodes. All the tiny kids, all the fat kids, all the kids with learning disabilities were put in Red House. Somehow it always fell to you to look after them and to pick them up when they fell over or to stop at the halfway point and wait for the pitiful Red House straggler to catch you up so that he or she wouldn't have to finish last and feel terrible. And you never stopped smiling, never minded not winning.

I can see you running over to us at lunchtime as we sat on our too small picnic rug surrounded by the likes of Sylvie and Terry James and the Wiggetts, all with their state-of-the-art, collapsible picnic furniture and go-faster cool boxes. Only Paul and Mel were less well equipped than us. They didn't even have a rug and for lunch they restricted themselves to cold Linda McCartney vegetarian sausages. Mummy used to bring you a tub of cherry tomatoes which you would eat one after another without stopping until they were gone.

In the afternoon when all three of you were still at the school, we would go and watch Robbie in the standing long jump, which was the only event in which he ever competed. Personally I am not sure that it is an event and I have never heard of it before or since. We would all watch and try not to laugh as Robbie, motionless and a study in concentration, would suddenly leap forwards, propelled up to three feet by his powerful, sticklike legs. The whole thing was over in less than a second. Robbie was worn out and mentally drained by the challenge.

I remember your mortification when I succumbed to Mrs Dunn's taunts and agreed to compete in the fathers' race. You ran away and hid behind the Portakabin, your face blending perfectly with the brilliant red of your T-shirt. Alan Wiggett stripped off his outer garments to reveal streamlined running shorts and running shoes with spikes. I took off my shoes and socks and ran in bare feet and jeans. I came last and nearly had a heart attack. I had hoped that you would be proud of me but you said that I was a hideous embarrassment and that I was to keep out of your way for the rest of the day.

Disturbing us from our dreams, Kate came to get us and we walked into the hall where, upon seeing us, all the teachers, pupils and parents stood and clapped. I stared at the floor. I'm sure Mummy did too. I had thought that I would have to make a speech but in the end there was not time. A girl won. I am afraid I cannot remember her name. Mummy and I shook her hand and I said, 'Well done' to her, not really knowing what else to say. I was terrified that I was going to drop your trophy but I didn't and we sat down, surrounded by the applause for the winner of the first Charlie Thompson trophy. I was sad that I couldn't make a speech. I had rehearsed in my head what I was going to say. I wanted to tell the children about you, to give them a sense of you. I was going to say that you found beauty and wonder in everything around you and that a vivid imagination is a great gift, a gift that you never wasted.

Something else happened last week. I have a letter on my desk from the chief executive of Network Rail, a man named John Armitt. In the letter he says that Network Rail has agreed to pursue certain actions to make Elsenham station safer. A ticket machine is going to be installed on the Cambridge platform, together with a 'second train coming' warning system with an experimental voice-over. They are going to launch a local awareness campaign including a briefing to local schools. They are also going to review the locking of the wicket gates. These changes are going to be made before the publication of the Rail Accident Investigation Board's report and before your inquest. Until recently they had made it very clear that there would be no changes until after your inquest and the publication of the report. Some people have said that we should be glad, that a victory has been won. I am glad in a way. Of course I am glad that now there is much less chance that any others will suffer as you have. How can I be glad, though, when this is a public admission that the station could have been safer? How can I be glad knowing that you should be here, looking over my shoulder, tormenting Horsey, filling the world with colour and joy and laughter?

There is, of course, no mention of a bridge. Maybe it will be possible to build one. There are many problems. The platforms are staggered, which means that the bridge would have to span the tracks and the road and it would

have to be high enough to clear the high voltage cables
that power the trains. This equates to a pretty big bridge
apparently, which would require some kind of central
supporting structure to stop it falling down. Then you
have to get permission from all the different authorities
and landowners. No problem is insurmountable but a
victory has been won. A horrible hollow victory at a
terrible cost.

It is half past five on Sunday afternoon. I have just come
in from the garden where Mummy has been replanting
the willow tree which you and she bought from Saggers,
the garden centre, last summer. Robbie has just come out
of the shower, which he undertook voluntarily. The heat
has driven him to cleanliness. Horsey and Cheese are
sitting together watching *Pirates of the Caribbean* in the
living room. We are meant to be going to France to stay
with the McPartlands in a little more than a week but I
have just discovered that Mummy's passport is out of date
and I have the distinct feeling that we won't be going
anywhere. I told Mummy about an hour ago and she
merely raised her eyebrows and said, 'Oh well.' Still, I'm
going to ring the passport office and see what can be
done.

At the moment I am a ship becalmed with no wind to
fill my sails. Each day is the same. I wake up to the
inevitability of your absence. I talk to you. I tell you I
love you. I kiss your photograph. I think about you all
the time. I am terrified of not thinking of you, of brief
periods when I am distracted by other thoughts. Uncle

Davy is the same. He feels guilty if he does not think of
Dan all the time. I constantly forget what I am supposed
to be doing. I go to the Spar or the Londis at least five
times a day because I always forget what it is I am meant
to be buying. The poor woman behind the counter
obviously thinks I'm insane or in love with her. I lose my
phone and the car keys, and I regularly leave my wallet on
the roof of the car. I know that I will have to change. I
know that I will have to find the strength to go forward,
to properly look after Mummy and Robbie and Horsey.
There are still terrible things that I will have to do, things
that I can't think about. One day we will have to go back
to Belchamp, to the churchyard. My blood runs cold at
the thought of next Christmas.

John Keeling said to me that there is only love and
hope. I love you so much. More than these words or any
words can ever say. I will never stop writing to you.
Never stop thinking of you. Oma says you are
everywhere. You are the wind in the trees, the sunlight
playing across the surface of the water, the rain, the snow
and the clouds. You are every blade of grass and the heart
of every flower. Sometimes I feel you so strongly that I
can believe that you are a part of me.

Bless you my darling.

Your Daddy

Acknowledgements

Sometimes I forget how our friends have suffered too, how they miss Charlie and how their troubles and private tragedies have been forgotten in the whirlwind of despair that has swept us all away. We are at the beginning of our journey but we would not have made it this far without the kindness, wisdom and generosity of all those mentioned in this book of letters.

Our friends would not want our thanks but I thank them nonetheless.

There are some I would like to mention by name because we have only really come to know them since Charlie's accident and they have helped us both spiritually and professionally. The Reverend Richard Titford, whose unshakeable faith in a 'guiding spirit' has brought us comfort. Dr Mike Tayler, who cares so much. Robbie Gladwell, who held on to us in the darkest of our darkest hours.

I would also like to pay tribute to my brother David and his wife Trish and their children Simon, Jamie and Francesca, who have suffered their own grievous loss but found within themselves the strength to comfort us. My mother, known as Oma, whose strength, wisdom and courage are unquenchable. My wife's sister Jill and her three wonderful sons, Toby, Patrick and Oliver for being there no matter what the circumstance. Also my own sister Franky, who is far away but would be with us if she could.

I would also like too to thank the Newport kids, who are always welcome in our house: Charlie McP, Cheese, Fleetwood, Sam, Gary, Chitson, Calvert, Connor, Matt, Spuggy, Clayden, Lou, Liv, Will and the rest.

To the Bazlintons, Chris and Tina, and their daughter Stevie we send our love and our hope.

Finally I would like to thank Ann McFerran of the *Sunday Times*, Lizzy Kremer of David Higham Associates and Eleanor Birne of John Murray (Publishers) for making this book possible.